THE OTHER SIDE OF
PASTORAL
MINISTRY

THE OTHER SIDE OF
PASTORAL
MINISTRY

USING PROCESS LEADERSHIP
TO TRANSFORM YOUR CHURCH

DANIEL A. BROWN

WITH BRIAN LARSON

Foreword by Jack Hayford

ZondervanPublishingHouse

Grand Rapids, Michigan

A Division of HarperCollinsPublishers

The Other Side of Pastoral Ministry
Copyright © 1996 by Daniel Brown and Craig Brian Larson

Requests for information should be addressed to:

 Zondervan Publishing House
Grand Rapids, Michigan 49530

Library of Congress Cataloging-in-Publication Data

Brown, Daniel Alan, 1953–
    The other side of pastoral ministry : using process leadership to transform
your church / Daniel A. Brown with Brian Larson.
       p. cm.
    Includes bibliographical references.
    ISBN: 0-310-20602-2 (pbk.)
    1. Christian leadership. 2. Pastoral theology. I. Larson, Craig Brian. II.
Title of Book.
BV652.1.B77 1996
253—dc20
                                                96-22620
                                              CIP

Interior design by Sherri L. Hoffman

Printed in the United States of America

96 97 98 99 00 01 02 03 /❖ DH/ 10 9 8 7 6 5 4 3 2 1

To my pastor, Jack W. Hayford,
who taught me that godly leaders
serve the plans of God and the people of God
by believing that both will
turn out great in the end

DANIEL A. BROWN

CONTENTS

FOREWORD

As I step over the boundary concluding my fourth decade in public ministry, an ever-deepening appreciation grips me whenever I witness spiritual leadership rising among the generation behind me.

I don't mean "leadership" in the general sense that pastors and workers are given to serve local assemblies and ministries at hundreds of thousands of locations. I refer to those men and women who are singularly touched by the hand of the Savior to be leaders among their peers.

No human hand can manipulate such recognition (and wisely, none would ever attempt it). So when, with the passing of time, a young man becomes recognized by fellow servants as a trusted spokesperson for his generation, it is a happy fact to be confirmed as a placement by God's hand, not man's. Such "gifts" to the Body, as *gifted* ones given by the Giver of ministry to His church (Eph. 4:8-11), are choices of God's grace. And it's that "grace" that explains the phenomenon that occasions some men realizing realms of influence exceeding the average.

But since such gifting *is* by grace, there is a sadness that too often besets the church. It occurs when anyone so gifted either exploits his privileged role to serve selfish ends, or defiles it by refusing to acknowledge that no degree of divine grace grants a leader the luxury of self-serving indulgence. The disciplines of full integrity to the Cross and the discipling call of our Savior are not only equally incumbent upon *all* who lead but uniquely to be expected of those "graced" to lead among leaders.

That is why I am especially happy to write these words at the front of this work designed to speak to pastoral leaders. Daniel Brown is a faithful disciple of Jesus, who not only has become respected as a leader among his peers these past few years but is also a servant-spirited shepherd whom I know to live out the fullest character requirements of godly leadership.

Daniel deserves to be heard for this reason, first of all, because he is more than merely *gifted*. When such commitment and character are also matched with such skill and insight as his leadership reveals, we all have reason to give time and thought to what these pages offer.

Further, for my own part, I have a distinct, personal joy. There are few things more gratifying than being called "Pastor"—among them, to be called a father. I am honored and humbled that Daniel Brown refers to me by both terms. Not only did I serve him as pastor during his college years, and later as a teammate when he joined our staff at The Church On The Way in the 1980s, but he and Pamela still call me that today. Among my personal letters I hold the treasure of a voluntary acknowledgment Daniel made to me after he had been in his own senior pastorate for years. His choice to call me "a father in the faith" meant much then and means even more now.

Today we are standing at a dramatic moment in the history of the church. There is a millennium beckoning us and a revival rising around us. In that environment, nothing is needed more than pastors and spiritual leaders who care about the fullest depths and dimensions of pastoral ministry. I heartily commend Daniel's words here to you—but more than that, I commend *him*. His words will profit you because they are born of extended, fruitful, pastoral enterprise. I think they will breathe *life* to you, as to me, because they flow from a heart of proven fidelity and constancy to the way of the Lord—as a man, as a husband, as a father, and as a shepherd.

JACK W. HAYFORD, D. LITT.
SENIOR PASTOR, THE CHURCH ON THE WAY
VAN NUYS, CALIFORNIA
JUNE 1996

ACKNOWLEDGMENTS

This book came together as a result of the encouragement of several important people. In its genesis, Bryan Feller, one of the key players at the Charles E. Fuller Institute, asked me to develop a seminar on my unconventional perspective on the nature of the local church and how to lead it.

Stan Gundry, now vice president and editor-in-chief of Zondervan Publishing House, was given two tapes of that seminar, and he flew to meet me for lunch three years ago to see if we could develop a book on the subject. His interest heartened and amazed me, but I just couldn't fit writing time into my schedule.

Then I met Brian Larson, contributing editor of *Leadership Journal*, who wanted to tackle the subject as a joint project. Our friendship has been a great reward. He edited and rearranged transcripts of the video seminar—enough to let me add any *other* thoughts I might have on the various components of church leadership. As it turned out, I had lots of *other* thoughts.

My staff, especially Merrilee Tunink (who had to type the manuscript as many times as I had to read it), has pulled for me and pitched in to help keep the church going. And my family cheered me on.

Throughout the entire writing process, I kept thinking of pastors who serve so selflessly and so diligently. The look in their eyes, the puzzlement in their hearts—these have kept me going.

Chapter One

THE POWER OF PROCESS

> And David shepherded them with integrity of heart;
> with skillful hands he led them.
>
> —Psalm 78:72

If you, as a church leader, have felt uncertain about where the Lord is leading the church in our culture—in this day and age—it's likely that you are accurately tuned into God. I don't mean that God is unsure of his plans and intentions, but that he has his church in a marvelous season of uncertainty, with everyone casting about trying to figure out what God is up to. You are not lost; neither are you alone. The ambivalence that you and church leaders all across the planet are experiencing are not signs of impending collapse; they are prophetic nudgings from a good and kind God. "Good and upright is the Lord," says Psalm 25; "therefore he instructs sinners in his ways" (v. 8). The rapidly shifting world has not taken God by surprise. Long ago he readied himself for this time in history, and he is prompting his church with counsel and instruction. Isn't it great to know we qualify for receiving that instruction?

How we think about our situation will usually end up shaping *what* we think about it. Since most of us who lead in the body of Christ sincerely devote ourselves to fulfilling his agenda instead of our own, we are desperate to know his will. We don't like being uncertain of his plan or unsure of ourselves. We want to know what he wants us to do.

But uncertainty can stem from more than one cause—and it isn't necessarily a negative condition. A leader whose sense of vision and direction requires constant reinforcement by the Lord may feel uncertain because of not hearing God's regular affirmation. A good God may be building that leader's stamina and confidence—not withholding approval. God isn't neglecting the leader's felt needs; he is taking care of the leader's future needs. Likewise, when God's kind intention is to alert his church to new things he wants to do, he may allow a measure of uneasiness and uncertainty in church leaders in order to motivate them to search out his new workings.

God loves us. He enjoys being with us and filling our lives. Sometimes I feel as though God is playing the same game with me that I used to play with my children—"Hot and Cold." I hid a quarter or a special gift in the family room, and then the kids scurried around hunting for it as I told them they were getting either "hotter, hotter, hotter" or "colder, colder, colder." Like a loving father who enjoys helping his kids, God wants to help us understand church ministry. But he wants us to find the treasure by listening to his voice, not just by frantically searching. Despite the uncertainties of our age, I hear him saying, "You're getting warmer." God is not toying with us. The Giver of the gift wants the pleasure of directing us to it.

NEW MODELS NEEDED

Most leaders acknowledge the need for fresh, innovative models of church—not new programs or theology, but models that explain the "parts" of church and how those components work together. When we attend conferences or visit successful churches, we are looking for models that will help us modify our approach to church ministry. We all have been guilty of trying to adopt another church's program or mission statement as a "quick fix." And we all have discovered that such pirating doesn't work for long. Learning why a church does something is always more useful than simply copying what that church does.

We know we need more fundamental changes in the way we think about and do church—not just in our programs and staffing but also in our very understanding of what this thing called *church* is supposed to do and be. We *have* churches—or at least we have a role in leading churches—but most of us do not clearly grasp what it is that we *have* in having a church. Too often we can be stuck in the forms we have always known and assume they are the New Testament model for the church. There is no single New Testament model for the church. Biblical passages about the church are vague, intentionally it seems, and most are descriptive rather than prescriptive.

When I was about to pioneer The Coastlands eleven years ago, I was all excited until I realized one day that I really didn't know for myself how a church was to be arranged. I wondered, *How do I do it? Where do I start, and what am I starting?* I went to the Bible and noted every reference to the structure, organization, and workings of the church. When I was finished with the New Testament, I looked at my hodgepodge of notes and tried to figure out how all the information went together. I finally figured out that there is no single prototype of the church.

This is a well-kept secret. Church members or other ministers will earnestly tell us, "We need to have a *New Testament* church." What does that really mean? What are the necessary conditions, the vital components that fully constitute such a church? What elements, if missing, prevent a church from being a New Testament church? When pressed for such a definition, no one will be able to offer a compelling outline for the illusive *New Testament church*.

Which New Testament church do you want to pastor? The one at Ephesus, Pergamum, Smyrna? How about Corinth? While there are some commonalties, the New Testament describes churches of different styles and approaches—just as we see in our day. While we must hold firmly to Scripture, we shouldn't be intimidated by this notion of *the* New Testament church. Based on our theological understanding of the church, we will want to develop a vision for the practical, organic church that will accomplish the Lord's calling today.

I have found that what people attending a church mean by a *New Testament* church is no more than the kind of church that agrees with their preexisting thinking about church. They mean a church that does what they want, how they want. Do they really want the sort of church in which the penalty for perjury is death (Acts 5:1–11); that is persecuted and scattered to other cities (Acts

8:1–8); that tolerates Jezebel (Rev. 2:20); or that confuses potlucks with Communion (1 Cor. 11:20–34)? New Testament churches are neither trouble-free, nor do they all look alike. People in churches blackmail pastors by appealing to an unimpeachable source—but they have attached *their* meaning to what that source says.

One church may be perpetually impoverished and under constant persecution (see Rev. 2:9) like a congregation I know in Athens. Their church services are translated into three different languages (Bulgarian, Polish, and Spanish) besides Greek, and they last for three hours! Another church may be situated in an area of especially active hellish influence (see Rev. 2:13) like a small congregation in the red-light district of Amsterdam to which our church has sent a missions team. And churches in decline that once were known for their dynamic ministry (see Rev. 3:1–2) are going to face different challenges than a pioneer church (see Acts 14:19–28). Whatever the church or cultural situation, good leadership can make a great difference in what the people in those churches experience. God has a set of instructions, a vision for intentional faith-filled leaders to grasp.

UNDER THE HOOD

My purpose in writing this book is not to lay out a blueprint or a paint-by-number diagram for a successful church. Rather, I am offering language and perspectives that will enable you to rethink the many dimensions of church—its parts and process—and how better to configure those components in order to fulfill the mission Jesus has given to you. If we don't understand the inner workings of the church, we are destined to frustration and perhaps failure. Like King David, we need not only integrity and spirituality to lead the people of God, we need specific skills.

"Skillful hands" (Ps. 78:72) in the Hebrew refers to reason and intelligence that comes from understanding everything that is involved in making a decision. Having considered and analyzed each of the component parts, the leader adopts a specific position. A skillful leader prudently discerns what is going on; much wisdom comes from analysis and good thinking. Not all wisdom is spiritual.

Our ability to analyze our church situation is severely limited
because we generally lack the language and the know-how to identify the many different moving parts in this thing called *church*.
Beyond study skills for sermon preparation, we need people skills,
ministry skills, and leadership skills.

We might even call this book "Church Mechanics 101." As
with most people who drive cars, we pastors know little about
what is going on "underneath the hood" of our church. We may
know where to stick in the key, where to pour in the gas, where we
want to go, and how to obey the laws of the road, but if our engine
rattles, we have no idea how to fix it. We keep driving until our car
wobbles uncontrollably or finally dies on some expressway.

People like me, who know next to nothing about how cars
work, follow a roadside ritual when our car dies. We get out and
walk around it as though, somehow, our survey of the situation
will help. Maybe we look at the tires—at least we can see them.
We bend over and glance under the car a time or two hoping the
problem will be obvious. Eventually we work our way around the
car and open the hood. We wiggle a few belts, try to tighten a few
caps, and stare uncomprehendingly at the engine. Finally, we
decide to wait for a tow truck.

As we loiter in front of that stalled automobile, passing cars—
running cars—look very attractive. *When I get a new car,* we
think, *I'd like one that color. And next time I'll buy a different
make or model, because this one is a lemon.* We assume the
answer to our problem is a new car, so we ask the tow truck driver
to pull our car into the denominational used-car lot. We want
someone else to fix our car or we want someone else's car.

Churches, like cars and bodies, work much better and last a
lot longer if we take care of them. Granted, it's possible our
church problem is mostly spiritual. If we're lacking in prayer and
discipleship and aren't following the Spirit, no amount of leadership or organizational understanding will lead the church into
effectiveness for Christ. "Unless the Lord builds the house," says
Psalm 127, "its builders labor in vain" (v. 1). Investing our energies in the parts and processes, the organic dimension of the
church will accomplish nothing for the kingdom if we are not

activated by the Spirit of God—even if we succeed in building a big church.

Most church leaders, however, do sincerely seek the Lord. We do our best to drive where he has told us to drive. We pray, fast, and read God's Word with an open ear and heart. Still, we face tremendous frustration in leading the church. The car keeps stalling or veering to the right or guzzling unbelievable amounts of personal energy. Why? Because church leaders have been trained to do a great job at one half of leadership, the "spiritual" side, but they have been ill-informed about or have neglected or despised the organic side—organization, systems, and processes. Excelling at spiritual things doesn't always make the natural issues go away. No matter how much we pray and give money to the needy, for example, if we don't brush our teeth, we'll get cavities; if we don't maintain our homes, they'll fall apart; if we don't put money in our checking accounts, our checks will bounce.

Many church leaders fall short of their dreams because they fail to fully appreciate the dual nature of ministry—that it is both spiritual and natural. Many veer toward one of the extremes, either being spiritually idealistic or pragmatically technique driven. Ministry that recognizes both the spiritual and natural dimensions is the sort of skillfulness that David had.

This book assumes that you as a church or ministry leader are already seeking the heart of Father God and are eager for everything he wants. You have taken Personal Ministry 101, 201, and 401. What you need is Church Ministry 101, 201, and 401. You sense you need help with the organic process of ministry, which involves both the natural and spiritual dimensions. Rather than offering you a management-style book filled with time lines, organization techniques, schedule suggestions, or planning principles, this book will give you an entirely different way to think about church. The change in your thinking will automatically lead to changes in your leadership approach to church.

THE RIVER

To help us understand how we can be more effective with the organic side of church life, let's change the metaphor. Our models—

how we think about what makes church and what makes it work—largely determine how we lead, what results we have, and what conclusions we reach. If we are not satisfied with our results and conclusions, we may have a need for new models, paradigms, ways of thinking. God is not scolding us for not having gotten with the program thus far. He isn't just urging us to be more contemporary with our society. He wants to instruct us for the new season before us.

What is church? How should we think about it to become more effective in leading it? To begin answering this simple question, I want to introduce the theme of this book—a perspective that we will come back to over and over: Church is a process like a river, not a static place like a lake. As church leaders adopt an understanding that church is an ongoing process, they will become more effective.

Both a lake and a river provide scenic beauty, and if our only purpose for them is as objects to be painted, then one is as good as the other. But rivers and lakes work very differently. Lakes are fairly limited in what they can do: grow or shrink. Rivers, however, go somewhere; they change and move on. Though made of the same stuff as lakes, rivers have a momentum that transports people and goods—to take them farther along than where they first joined the river. And rivers can change course, an option available only to moving things.

God changes the course of history and the course of people's lives. He transforms us in an ongoing process of metamorphosis and sanctification. God does more than just grow or shrink us; he leads us and directs our course. Life with him is an ongoing process, not a static condition. To think more like him, we must become process thinkers. Process thinking is kingdom thought. It transforms our church, not necessarily into a significantly larger congregation but into a significantly more fruitful congregation. In a kind letter to me from a church family moving out of our area, a woman wrote, "I want to thank you for the opportunity to attend your church for these years. My whole life has been transformed."

"Actually," she continued, "ninety percent of the change in my life has come through the work of my cell-group leader." She went on to describe how the cell leader had ministered to her family in various ways. She closed with, "Thank you for having cell groups and putting me in touch with this leader." After signing her name, she added, "P.S. Who would have guessed that my life could have been transformed by a sheet metal worker?"

This woman's story testifies to the power of process. First, her life had truly been transformed. She could identify numerous "course changes" in her life. She was headed in a different direction than before. Second, she didn't enthuse about my speaking or the great special events at The Coastlands. What touched her was the ministry of the people in her cell group—one part of the strategic process at The Coastlands designed to reach a clearly defined goal: to patch up hurting people and get them healthy enough to patch up others. At The Coastlands we know what we want to happen in people's lives, and we have designed a process to accomplish that.

Viewing church as a river, a current, and a process, focuses on development, not just a final measurement of growth. The river model is a developmental model. Process thinking targets the change in people as the whole point of church: no matter how many people are "in process" and no matter where they are in that process, a church can be successful if it keeps developing those people. People in a lake swim back to shore to retrieve their towels and belongings—the same shore from which they entered the lake. River-goers don't have that luxury (temptation), because the current has taken them farther than they were when they got in the water.

Unintentionally, leaders often have approached church as though it were a lake rather than a river. Church becomes a place to collect more and more people—as many as possible. Success is measured more by the size of the lake than by what happens to people in it. Even if the lake is growing, it is often static, without currents, lacking direction for how members should progress in faith. If someone leaves the church, leaders interpret it as a loss, a failure (unless the person enters vocational ministry). In the lake model, the key to personal growth is attendance: the more time someone spends in the lake, it is assumed, the more mature that person becomes. The process model, on the other hand, celebrates the change that happened in the person's life *while* that person was in the river. The point is not returning to the point of entry, but being taken farther along the way. The lake model forces leaders to focus large amounts of attention on material things like buildings and programs—elements of church to which people can come. Attendance at meetings, not necessarily growth in character and service, becomes the goal. The lake swimmers are counted; their progress is rarely measured.

A pastor's desire to have a bigger church or a better attended vacation Bible school is not, as many have misinterpreted it, necessarily an unrighteous, greedy desire. Some insecure pastors may want the numbers simply to boast, but most pastors focus on numbers as a measure of how successful their churches are. A poor showing at a prayer rally marks the event as a flop: "Only seventeen showed up. What a shame; we had such a great program lined up." This is where the difference between church as a lake and church as a river becomes apparent. *How many people were there?* is lake thinking. *What happened to those who were there?* is river thought.

HOW WAS CHURCH?

Because we have church services on Saturday night and Sunday morning, my wife (who usually attends Sunday) asks me every Saturday night, "How was church?" She doesn't mean *How many people attended?* She means *What happened?* Actually, she is as much interested in any conversations I had with people before or after the service as she is in the service itself. She wants to know how people are and if they were helped, touched, comforted, and encouraged *by what happened*.

When we see church as a process of touching people and transforming them, it shifts our focus away from the programs, the building sites for those programs, and the staff needed to maintain those buildings and programs. "Did the program 'get to' (affect) the people?" replaces the question, "How many people 'got to' (attended) the program?" thus revealing the goal of the church.

In lake churches, events are usually unrelated, chiefly designed to attract more people, and as a result, these events aren't integrated into a growth process. These unrelated events are more calendar driven than process driven: during the summer a church scales down a bit; at Christmas they have a bathrobe pageant. And at Easter there is a sunrise service. Nothing is wrong with such events, but the approach is random—or shaped by the goal of increasing attendance.

Goals, purpose, mission—these are words we have read a lot about over the past fifteen to twenty years in church leadership circles. They are important, but before we can have a meaningful mission statement for our church, we must resolve this more fundamental issue: What does a "good job" mean? What are we really trying to do with church?

If an unchurched person overheard two lake-thinking pastors talking about how church was going, that person might picture a whirlpool. Much of the pastors' conversation would revolve around how to get people from the fringes into the core. But in the river model, people don't have to be in the center to go somewhere. If they just get in the river, even at the edge, they will be taken somewhere. I'm constantly asking myself, "Where will people in The Coastlands be taken as a result of being in the church?" Just getting them into the church is no big deal if they aren't taken somewhere. But getting people in a river is always significant, for people who get in a river only once in a while are taken farther than those who swim often in a lake. River-thinking leaders aren't very concerned about a core-group/fringe-group distinction, because there is simply too much volatility both at the core and the fringe today for such an idea to be realistic. But if people are connected with a process-model church in any way, the current will carry them along.

What effect will process thinking actually have on how we "do" church? When planning something like a Christmas play, for example, the interest in a process church will not be primarily on the production itself. Rather, process thinkers will see a great opportunity for discipling the people involved in the play as they prepare for it. A Christmas pageant draws people together for several weeks. The excitement of new experiences, new friends, and deadlines creates an atmosphere wherein the participants can grow spiritually. The conversations and crises, the relationships, the stress, and the rewards will come together as a curriculum of transformation. When the pageant is over, the participants ought to be more affected than the audience. Table 1.1 contrasts the emphases of the two models.

Table 1.1
Basic Elements of Church

Static "Lake" Model	Process "River" Model
Building	Environment
Place for people to attend	Process to tend people
Series of unconnected events	Strategic systems
More people	Growing people
Individual attendance	Individual involvement
Performance	Training
Events to attract people	Events to shape people

No leader consciously puts more emphasis on the items in the static column, but that is where our priorities and resources can unintentionally fall. The static model is a spiritual cul-de-sac.

WHAT'S YOUR JOB, ANYWAY?

I recall a painful time some years ago when I drove unintentionally into that cul-de-sac. I hit a dead end. I could get no further with my lake-thinking. What happened to me became the pivotal experience that forever changed my thinking about church. We had been losing people from the church for several months, and my discouragement came to a head one Sunday after service. The morning had been a disaster. The people straggled in and sat, scattered all over the auditorium. The ushers had filled in the gaps between people with latecomers. The worship was flat— I think only the worship team sang above a whisper. And as I readied to deliver the sermon, only one thought crossed my mind: *Who are you people, and what have you done with my congregation?*

I had invested so much in people who no longer went to our church. Six months ago we were a model church, filled with maturing saints. Now we were a fragmented hodgepodge. *I quit,* I thought. *I'm a failure. This isn't working.*

Out of nowhere, I sensed a cheerful, matter-of-fact question pressing in on the edges of my discouragement. It was as though someone who could not appreciate the gravity of my situation just showed up and asked me, *What is your job anyway?*

I'm supposed to make disciples, I responded to the internal question.

Then (depending on your theology) the "inner voice" or God said, *That's right, and I think you have done a very good job.*

I was shocked. That's why I know this was God—no matter what your theology is—because I never would have come to the conclusion myself that I was doing a good job. I was trying to resign my commission, not pump myself up.

The cheerful, "Isn't-it-a-great-day?" voice pressed on: *Haven't you noticed how many people I've taken out of your church lately?*

Are you kidding? I thought. We had shifted the church's emphasis to cell groups, and people had been bailing out like nobody's business. Our total attendance remained around eight hundred, because new people were coming in, but one in five of the adults who had been significant participants in the church for three to four years had left us. And I was getting a little nervous about it. I wanted to tell the voice it should have asked me the haven't-you-noticed-people-leaving question first. Then it would have known that all this "good job" nonsense was inappropriately spoken to a failure like me.

I told you that you've done a good job. You have discipled these people, and now I have use for them elsewhere. I have given you a new group of people, and it's your job to teach people who don't know me well to know me better.

Anyone watching me at that moment would have witnessed my face jerking suddenly toward the sky—half in defiance *(Who said that? Let me decide for myself whether or not I have failed)* and half in humbled conviction. I had been nailed.

Within an instant, I was fully convicted of the wickedness in my heart. My idea of church had been a place that was finished, filled with people who were near perfect and had no issues to deal with. If other pastors visited The Coastlands, I wanted them to think, *So this is The Coastlands. Daniel Brown. I heard him at a seminar. Nice church.* That was my idea of church, yet it was the kind of church I had failed to have. I certainly hadn't learned of that kind of church in the Bible. But somewhere I had bought into a production model of church that is evaluated on the quality of its show, its actors, and its audience. I had no understanding of process. I wanted my people developed and matured because it was easier. I had forgotten that my calling was to develop the undeveloped, to mature the maturing.

I had been a lake-thinker. I thought I could judge the quality of a church by attending a service and observing the actors and the spectators. I have since learned process thinking, river-thought, and I know that the quality of a church can be judged only by discovering how much further along it has taken its people since last month or last year.

We don't necessarily put on a highly polished performance at The Coastlands. We aren't sloppy, but our church is filled with people and even run by leaders who haven't arrived, and that's fine with me. We want a church where people who don't know God well can learn to know and serve him better. That gets messy. Since the day I heard God speaking to me, I have come to appreciate Proverbs 14:4: "Where there are no oxen, the manger is empty, but from the strength of an ox comes an abundant harvest."

The messiness bothers many "mature Christians" who have grown accustomed to an established order. They feel comfortable returning to their towels on the lakeshore. They like the idea that only a gifted few ought to be trusted with meaningful ministry. That may be why many of the eighty to one hundred adults left our church when we began resourcing and releasing "average" people in small-group leadership ministry.

PROCESS THINKING IS RISKY

Shortly after the "I'm a failure" episode, God punctuated his assignment to me with another life-changing encounter. This time, however, my conversation was not with the Lord but with a couple in our church. I'll call them the Donovans. The Donovans are godly people who deposited untold wealth and wisdom into our young congregation. As older believers, they gave stability and credibility to many younger people in our church. Perhaps it was the age difference or their more traditional sense of how church ought to be run that led to their decision to leave our church. And the degree to which I loved the Donovans (and they, me) only made the separation of our ways more poignant.

I will never forget our last meeting. As often happens when there are deep differences in thinking about church, a slight unease had come between the Donovans and me. Small things, wording, matters of no consequence became skirmishes that foreshadowed greater conflict. They made an appointment with me to warn me about the unqualified condition of my cell leaders.

Some months earlier I had asked them to help me disciple some of our newer cell-group leaders by visiting them and teaching at the cell-group meetings. They were not willing to be cell leaders themselves, and they could not, in confidence, come under the care of these novice leaders in our church. The Donovans felt great apprehension over what might happen when unqualified people "got hold of the Bible and the Holy Spirit."

I acknowledged that we all need more nurture and development, and I rehearsed with them the pathetic inadequacy of the first Bible studies I had led in college. "And you," I asked, "were you always this qualified, or did someone give you a chance to get started?"

Then I proposed a solution. Instead of leaving our church for good, maybe they could just go away for a year or two. "Because," I said, "you know that we will work with these leaders and disciple them into the kind of leaders you are looking for." I paused for a few moments before I realized this was a defining moment in my ministry. I continued, "But that solution probably won't work. With my passion to keep raising up people into ministry, when you come back in a year or two, you will most likely end up in a cell group led by another 'unqualified' leader."

I'm sure the Donovans are contributing to some church somewhere, because that's the kind of people they are. But I can't help but feel sad to know how much they have missed by not being here to help and to watch the "unqualified leaders" become men and women of incredible spiritual substance and experience. Like absentee parents, they are missing the joy of seeing their "kids" grow up. Those previously "unqualified leaders" are working with our current "unqualified leaders."

We are in a developmental process that is never finished; as God brings people into the church, we work with them, and then in a few years many of them move on to something else God has for them. The Coastlands is like a way station on the old stage-coach lines. Few of us live here, but many are refreshed and resourced here. Central to our vision is starting new churches. To date, we have started fourteen churches in just over eleven years.

AN ORGANIZED SOCCER TEAM

My two boys have played lots of organized soccer, and I was their coach for many years. When coaching six- and seven-year-old soccer players, it is important to think through what the kids can and should learn. There are no World Cup stars at that age. We began with basics like simply kicking the ball—which isn't easy for small children. In a game, after little kids kick the ball, their first reaction is to proudly look over at Mom and Dad and wave, as if to say, "I did it! I kicked the ball!"

After they master kicking the ball, we move up to kicking the ball two or three times in a row. All along we're teaching them to kick it in the right direction. Several seasons ago one boy got the ball on a breakaway; he couldn't believe how open he was. He kicked it once, he kicked it twice. Nobody was in front of him except the goalie. This was his moment of glory—he was going to score a goal! He didn't hear everyone on the sidelines screaming, "You're going the wrong way!" I wasn't worried, though. I knew that in under-eight soccer no kid can kick the ball more than three times in a row. Sure enough, when he tried to kick the ball on net, he missed the ball completely.

Just last year our under-twelve team (ages ten and eleven) ended up with a record of five wins and seven losses. That's not great, but our record doesn't tell you the whole story: we notched four of our five wins in the last five games. That's a record I can live with. We started the kids where they were—unsure at times where that was—and developed their skills until they won most of their games. Which is the better coach—the one whose team consists of several returning stars from last year and ends with a record of nine and three, or a coach who instills in even the not-so-gifted players a feeling of accomplishment and posts a five and seven season?

Youth soccer teams and churches can't really recruit players. So the issue for coaches and pastors is the same: How can we do the most with the players we have? There is no point in complaining about the kids on the team. Most of the other coaches have the same sort of roster. Coaching an organized team for a twelve-game season is entirely different from putting together a pickup game of kids on the block featuring star players. In the pickup game, the focus is on immediate performance, not on training; the only thing that matters is winning today. Organized coaching, on the other hand, is a developmental process over time. And so is church leadership. In a process-oriented church, we don't have to feel that all is lost if we have some failures. We have a process that will eventually take us where we need to be. Process leadership is a forgiving system focused more on training than on performing. It measures success by looking at the entire season—the training and developing of each player and the team as a whole.

DESIGNING THE PROCESS

At The Coastlands we think in terms of a three-year season. Most pastors don't want to plan on people's leaving their churches, but the reality in many places is that the majority of even regular attenders will move on in five to seven years. We don't have forever to shape people. If we conduct ministry as though everybody in our church today will always be in our church, we will have no sense of urgency and no purposeful design. But if we live with the prospect that most people in our church will sooner or later scatter around the world, then we have greater incentive to develop them so they are ready to go and be fruitful. By getting everyone ready for possible departure, we ensure that those whom God does keep in our church are brought to a place of strength and great fruitfulness.

To effectively design a process, we must start with the end result we seek. All church leaders want to develop mature Christians, but that's far too general to help us plan the process. We need to specifically define the desired results. What growth do we want in the areas of ministry skills and experiences, understanding of Scripture and theology, spiritual disciplines, use of money, sensitivity to the Spirit's leading, use of leisure time, ability to share Christ with the unchurched, ability to serve Christ at work?

Though I view church as a process, I see it as a *terminal* process. I am constantly motivated by a dream in my heart. In the dream I have for the people of my church, I picture each of our church families moving to another town. I want those family members to be the most spiritual people on their block or in their apartment complex, to be able to start a home Bible study to teach their neighbors about the love of Jesus Christ, and to be able to minister to almost anyone's spiritual need. If they move away from our church, I want our people to be equipped and determined to equip others wherever they go. I live for that dream and design our church process toward that end.

After pastors and church leaders know the results they want, they must assess where the congregation is with respect to those end results: What do the congregants know? What is their Christian experience? What is their gifting? What are their sins, their needs and weaknesses, their strengths?

Finally, a process and systems can be designed to take people from where they are now to where the pastor and leaders perceive they should be in three to five years.

Table 1.2 offers an example of an exercise we can do ourselves and with other church leaders (this book will benefit your church most if *all* the leaders read and discuss it together). On a sheet of paper or blackboard, make three columns labeled *Abilities Now, Essential Parts of the Process,* and *Abilities in Three Years.* There are many things to develop in people, such as character traits and spiritual knowledge, but in this exercise we will focus primarily on the *abilities* we would like our people to have in their lives. Start with the last column (Abilities in Three Years) and list a few of the capabilities you want your people to have by the time they leave your church to accept some ministry assignment. Then try to identify at least two experiences that will help people develop each of their abilities. For instance, the first ability I have listed in our example—to forgive—will probably not develop unless the people (1) see the link between unforgiveness and personal misery, and (2) experience being forgiven.

Once you have identified the experiences people need to develop these abilities, you will have specific program ideas for the

---

Table 1.2

Abilities Now	Essential Parts of the Process	Abilities in Three Years
		Able to:
		1. Forgive others
		2. Worship freely
		3. Witness
		4. Serve unselfishly
		5. Give cheerfully
		6. Offer encouragement
		7. Lead Bible study
		8. Receive correction
		9. Accept thanks
		10. Pray over others
		11. Discern spiritual traps
		12. Overcome addictions
		13. Control the tongue

---

church. Continuing with our example, if you want people to learn about forgiveness, you can select sermon texts that refer to the misery of unforgiveness, such as the story of the unjust steward who was thrown in prison for not forgiving the small debt owed to him. For people to experience forgiveness, they will need to confess their sins to God, and they may need the reassurance of confessing to another person whom they can trust. For that kind of trust to be built, people will need quality heart-sharing time together. For them to have that kind of time.... On and on process thinking goes, taking you backward from the goal through the essential elements of the process. Process thinking realizes that most of what needs to happen in people won't just happen on its own or in an instant. The process must be directed and cultivated over time by skillful leaders.

SIX ADVANTAGES OF PROCESS LEADERSHIP

A process mentality suits any size church on any budget. We don't have to grow a church to a certain level before we can begin growing people. Once we know the processes that will take our people from where they are to where we want them to be, we can begin instituting those developmental elements and have a sense of accomplishment and movement on the very first day.

Process churches don't depend on great performances. With the developmental model we can weather a lot of bombs, failures, and mistakes because we haven't staked everything on the actors not forgetting their lines. For leaders with only average speaking skills or in churches with fewer resources, who aren't necessarily going to pull off an exceptional event time and time again, process leadership is the realistic route to take.

Process-oriented churches reflect our individual walks with God. Individual growth in God is an ongoing process. Churches cannot significantly affect something that is so clearly a process with a nonprocess orientation. We walk with the Lord, we are being sanctified, he is changing us—these are processes, not productions.

Process churches are less materialistic. They are less dependent on money. If life in God is spiritual, affected by the wind we can't see, which rustles the leaves we can see, then our church program ought to be more invisible and intangible. Money is not the answer to success.

Process leaders aren't always scrambling to find workers. Process churches focus on training workers rather than on finding talented "stars" who can perform well with little coaching. We don't mind taking in someone as a rookie who won't excel for a few years, because in the past we have worked with other rookies who now are carrying the load. Developmental churches enjoy delayed gratification.

Process leadership applies the principle found in Matthew 25:21: "You have been faithful with a few things; I will put you in charge of many things." If we have a static notion of leadership, we're just looking around for somebody who can do the job right now; we don't have time to think about building people up by giving them smaller tasks along the way. The process church is built on the idea of patiently bringing people along.

When people grow, the organization grows. Instead of accumulating more and more dependent people, process churches develop mature, fruitful Christians who strengthen the church with their finances, prayer, work, and involvement.

SORTING THE PILES

A famous anthropological study done many years ago in South America sought to discover how primitive cultures mentally sorted objects—according to shape or color. The purpose of the study was to look at linguistic priorities and the effects of thinking styles on societal structures. Researchers placed before various people a pile of squares, circles, triangles, and rectangles of different colors: red, yellow, green, and blue. They asked the people to divide the objects into piles.

People of some cultures sorted the objects according to color, and people of other cultures sorted according to shape. One group that sorted the objects according to color did something curious. They combined the blue and green shapes in one pile. The anthropologists wondered why. Later they discovered that in the language of that culture, there was a single word for both blue and green—just as English has but one word for the love of a friend and the love of a spouse.

As this study shows, language can blur ideas and limit our understanding and discernment, or it can sharpen them. Language and the categories words represent shape how we think and see our world. If someone asks us, "How's your church doing?" and the only way we know how to respond is in terms of attendance—"Great! Our attendance is up!" or "Miserable! We're losing people"—then our understanding of the processes in our church is woefully primitive.

In the following chapters we will look at several tributaries that feed the large river called *church*. By looking at how churches can work more purposefully, I want to enhance the skill of godly, Spirit-led leaders—to help you with the other half of leadership.

Chapter Two

BUILDING AUTHORITY

As we have already seen, the local church—its parts and how they work together—is more complex than the simple word *church* might convey. The same is true for the nature of leadership. Leadership, like church, is better understood as a process rather than as a series of static, unconnected episodes of leading. As with all the dynamics of church, leadership has two sides, the *organic* (which occurs naturally in any human organization) and the *spiritual* (which plays the larger part in a church). In their zeal to be spiritually correct, church leaders may inadvertently overlook important elements of an effective church ministry by trying to make all problems—and their solutions—spiritual. In the following pages we will spend little time on the spiritual side of leadership, not because it is insignificant but because the Bible covers that, and because I assume that you are doing everything you know to seek the Lord and his power. Spiritual integrity and godly character are the basis for effectively using the principles of this book.

Spiritually lackadaisical pastors, or those who compromise the truth of God's Word, will hinder their congregations. We know that. But that is exactly what frustrates most of us who pastor; we presume that the converse of that axiom ought to be true as well: If we do not compromise the truth, and if we are diligent, then our churches ought to flourish. What plagues most of us pastors are not dilemmas of ethics or doctrine, yet we keep finding ourselves stuck with churches that are not flourishing. So how can we be better leaders for the sake of the people in our churches?

Many pastors who are deeply spiritual falter at church leadership because they fail to appreciate the natural side of the equation—the organic issues that resist our best attempts at applying spiritual solutions. For instance, the reason that young families visit the church but don't stay may be an issue to resolve through prayer, but the problem might also be due to inadequate children's facilities or to children's programs that are rendered ineffective because key leaders in the church want to fill more *spiritual* and rewarding roles than working with children.

Pastors who preach powerful, life-changing sermons do not necessarily remember to inspire the nursery workers with "thank-yous" that let those workers know what a vital part they play in the overall ability of the church to affect people so profoundly.

We know that spiritual disorder and moral sloppiness will diminish ministry effectiveness in any church—sooner or later. But so will organizational weakness and administrative laxness. It is a challenge for leaders to pursue excellence in both the organic and the spiritual arenas, making sure they do not neglect or mistake the one for the other. When the Hellenistic widows were not getting their proper allotment of food, the apostles recognized the problem for what it was and solved it *organically*.

As we turn our focus to the nature of local church leadership, let us look at how many of the organic parts of that leadership process can be understood and improved upon. Leadership is more than a spiritual gift bestowed on certain people such as physical attribute or the gift of mercy. It can be learned and developed by those of us who want to become better church leaders.

THE NATURE OF AUTHORITY

One critical area of the leadership process that has both a natural and spiritual side is authority. How do pastors establish their authority in the eyes of others? Is authority a question of thunderous oratory, privileged parking places, or congregational size? What is its source and its purpose?

The basis of biblical leadership is true authority, and Jesus set the example for the kind of authority a church leader ought to have. People listened to Jesus because he taught the people "as one who had authority, and not as their teachers of the law" (Matt. 7:29). He did not teach them as he did the scribes or Pharisees, who knew a lot of Scripture but did not understand the heart or the purposes of God. When Jesus spoke, people sensed that he knew what he was talking about and that he knew how to piece lives together. The best way to define authority as it is used by Jesus in the Scriptures is "having insight, facility, or expertise" in matters relating to the kingdom of God. Just as a business hires consultants who are experts in their field, so too, do individual believers search for people whom they believe have special understanding of the things of God.

If a pastor wants to buy a church its first computer but doesn't know a thing about them, he would be unwise to drive to his local computer store and say, "Hi, I'm a pastor, and I want to buy a computer." They would sell him one, but it might be much more or much less computer than he needs. That pastor would be better off seeking the help of someone in the congregation who knows about computers. Likely he will discover, as I did, a person in the church who has tremendous background and expertise with computers and who is eager to be of help. The point of talking to an expert is that he or she can listen to what you need and match your needs with what is available in the computer world.

When people make important decisions, they seek help from an authority. We will be able to recognize whether or not we have authority in someone's life when he or she seeks our opinion. Our authority is something others perceive, not something we insist upon. Just because we hold a position of authority doesn't mean our opinions carry authority. The question is, Do people want to know what we think?

Credibility is built over time as one truly becomes a leader in the things of God. As we search the Word of God, we can begin to share with our congregation what we learn, and as time passes, people will begin to think, *This pastor knows what he's talking about*. The more credible we become, the more others come to us. Notice that it is both the passage of time and the seeking of answers from the Lord that builds our credibility with people.

One man served as a pastoral trainee at my church and about a year later became one of our associate pastors. After a month in his new role, he came to my office, looking quite perplexed and discouraged. He said, "I always thought that once I became a pastor, everybody would treat me differently. But they treat me just the same as they did before I was a pastor."

"You thought you would have new status?" I asked. "And that everyone would want your counsel?"

"Yes, I guess I did."

"I'm sorry to tell you this, but it doesn't work that way."

Back then my associate, who now knows better, had a faulty understanding of how and from where leaders derive their authority. He is not alone. A person can pastor for decades yet lack authority because he doesn't understand the nature of leadership and authority.

Our perception of leadership controls our understanding of the grounds for our authority. The purpose of authority is never to establish position over others, never to tear people down, to dominate them, or to lord over them in a way that would get them to do what the one in authority wants them to do. Those in authority should never be self-seeking and ought never to expect others to do what they are unwilling to do.

Some leaders mistakenly think of "taking authority over" people. The New Testament describes only two things over which we are told to take authority: *ourselves* (if more people took authority over themselves, they wouldn't need to "take authority" over so many other things) and *demonic forces*. Our congregations are neither of these. When we have spiritual authority with others, they recognize it and want to listen to what we say, and they follow us willingly.

Putting it another way—godly authority does not control people. Rather, godly authority so recommends itself to people because of its insight and understanding, its facility with the Word of God, that they seek to control themselves in response to the wisdom and understanding of that authority. Just as we are told to submit ourselves, so are we told to control ourselves, but the Bible never hints at the prospect of making others submit to us or having us control them.

I am not saying that the Bible only casually recommends submission as a take-it-or-leave-it suggestion. Hebrews 13:17 makes clear that we should submit to our leaders. But that counsel—like the counsel for wives to submit to their husbands and each of us to submit to one another—affirms a posture I should take toward those to whom I submit, not toward those God may ask to submit to me.

Submission is an act of obedience to God, not an act of subservience to people. It offers me an opportunity to empty myself and voluntarily follow Jesus' example of humbling myself (see Phil. 2:3–8). It does not grant to my leaders the license to empty or control me.

Leaders are servants. Leaders are to submit to the needs of those they are leading, making sure that they have done everything they can to see those needs met. They do this by being obedient to Jesus and by sacrificing themselves just as husbands are told to give themselves up for their wives (Eph. 5:25–29). When leaders love their people more than they love themselves, they are truly leading them.

Leaders don't issue commands. They offer input and perspective to people. The people must evaluate the advice for themselves. The better a leader's advice is over the years, the more people will probably follow it.

The purpose of true authority is to build people. Paul spoke of "the authority the Lord gave me for building you up, not for tearing you down" (2 Cor. 13:10). The acid test of spiritual authority is how many people we have built up in Christ.

ALENA AND LESTER

Alena and her husband, who had been attending our church for nearly five years, were thinking about leaving. They were friends with a couple who had left our church because of their unhappiness with me, and I could feel Alena and Lester's pulling away. Because I prefer to err on the side of *releasing* people rather than *constricting* them, I usually let people leave the church without attempting to dissuade them, but sometimes I sense that I would not be serving them well to simply let them slip away from our church without at least letting them know that I am concerned. I try, at those times, to keep speaking into their lives. Until people do leave my congregation, I have that responsibility.

Pastors and leaders can and do fall prey to an unrighteous temptation to hold on to people in order to validate themselves or their ministry. That is wrong. But even those of us who try to celebrate the release of our congregants to other churches when called to do so by the Lord, know there are times when people's reasons for leaving aren't right. I felt that about Alena and Lester, and I sensed I had enough relationship capital with Alena for perhaps one more conversation. Since she was the main impetus for their developing ambivalence toward me, I arranged to meet with her briefly.

"I know you're thinking about leaving," I said to her. "As soon as you tell me, I'll pass on my pastoral mantle to [the disgruntled couple], and I'll entrust you to their safekeeping and to their spiritual insights for your life."

She gave me a surprised look.

"If you leave to go with them," I continued, "it means, in effect, that you are being pastored and discipled by this couple. You have made the choice that they have more to speak into your lives than I do. You have decided to follow them rather than me. I accept that, and I am ready to release you; so you tell me when I'm to pass on this mantle."

She got saucer-eyed and began shaking her head a bit.

"Before you do decide to ask them to disciple you, though," I said, "can I ask you a question? Have you checked their spiritual portfolio? Have you looked at the pictures, as it were, of the people-houses they have custom built? If you plan to ask a contractor to build a custom house, you want to ensure that contractor has already built some nice houses. You wouldn't say to a demolition contractor who tears down houses with wrecking balls, 'Come and build my house.'"

By this time Alena was leaning back in her chair and shaking her head no.

"Can you name even one person," I asked, "whom this other couple has built from ground zero into fully functioning members of the body of Christ?"

"No, I can't," she exclaimed.

"You know that I have developed and built several people in God, don't you?"

"Yes."

"Remember, Alena, just because someone can tear a building down doesn't mean he has the expertise to build it up. Anyone can take a sledgehammer and knock down a wall. It takes no special insight to be able to criticize a church or a pastor. The real question is, What expertise do they have to develop your walk with the Lord?"

Lester and Alena are elders in our church almost six years later.

The ability to build others up is crucial to cultivating our credibility and influence with them.

THE UNRIGHTEOUS TENDENCIES OF AUTHORITY

There are four tendencies into which people in authority can easily slip and which will ultimately replace their godly authority with earthly, natural, or demonic authority inappropriate in the kingdom (see James 3:13–18).

1. *To set ourselves above, rather than beneath, people.* Godly authority is meant to serve people, but after we serve those people, they come to have a measure of gratitude and thankfulness in their hearts for us because of the help God has allowed us to give them. Since people are sheep, they can easily become comfortable with having someone tell them what to do. A common tendency of people, as demonstrated by the children of Israel, is to want a king.

We must be vigilant to keep our authority beneath people where it can serve them, rather than above them, where it can tell them what to do. To put it another way, our authority should offer perspectives to people for their prayerful consideration without becoming so heavy-handed that they feel they have no legitimate opportunity to decline what we offer them.

2. *To want others to serve us, rather than to serve them.* Again, people who have been served by our insight or expertise often express their gratitude by a desire to do whatever they can for us. Such gratefulness and appreciation are both wonderful and normal, but there is a lurking danger if they are not kept in perspective. It is easy to grow accustomed to being served and to forget to keep serving. Our service to people leads to their thankfulness to us. Their gratitude should always follow our serving. Fresh acts of

servanthood should outpace and outnumber their expressions of appreciation.

Serving is more costly than being thankful. Ministry is exhausting work, but if we are not careful, we can forget that leaders are supposed to have the hardest job. The very cost we pay for the privilege to serve others can turn into a burden for which we feel we deserve special privileges. When we are in authority, we must be careful always to serve more than we are served.

3. *To draw attention to ourselves rather than to the Lord*. Having been given by the Lord a measure of authority and expertise in the things of the kingdom, we can easily forget that nothing we have is of ourselves. Paul constantly had to remind others that what he had was not of himself but of the Lord (see 1 Cor. 4:1–13). If we lose sight of this truth and begin to think that our natural ability, wisdom, and so on has done such a wonderful job in people's lives, then we will quickly lose our true authority.

Godly authority is quiet like Jesus, telling people to give their thanks to God. The point is that they have received ministry; the person who has done that ministry is secondary. In the name of leadership, we can succumb to the temptation to boast about the great counsel we gave or the incredible truth we shared. Even if such boasting is done silently in our hearts, God hears it with grief.

4. *To expect that we will be seated at the head of the table*. Jesus says that when we come into a banquet room, we should take the lowest place at the table. And then if the Lord chooses to promote us, he will bring us up to the head of the table. When leaders have so often been brought to the head of the table, they can forget Jesus' advice. When they walk into situations and simply presume that they will be brought to the head of the table, they miss the opportunity to let it be the Lord who positions them.

This presumption and arrogance can develop imperceptibly over time, and it is especially deadly to people in authority. Philippians 2:3–4 holds a great lesson for those in authority: "Do nothing out of selfish ambition or vain conceit, but in humility consider others better than yourselves. Each of you should look not only to your own interests, but also to the interests of others." True humility—always a mark of true authority—remains a bit surprised when signaled out as anything special. Jesus' eye was always on the Cross, for he knew his servant role was meant to cost his life, not privilege it.

THE FALSE NOTIONS OF LEADERSHIP

Along with these unrighteous tendencies of authority, there are four false notions of leadership that undermine our authority with others. By identifying what true leadership is not, it will be easier to redefine what it is.

First, *leadership is not performance*. Long before any of us received a calling from the Lord to become leaders in the body of Christ, we were exposed to numerous leadership experiences that, together, shaped the way we think. We learned one of the most profound lessons in leadership when we were very young by playing the game "Follow the Leader." If the first person in line lifts her hand, all those following behind are supposed to lift their hands in exactly the same way. Why do kids play that game? What gives them incentive to attempt the actions initiated by the leader? *Follow* is another word for *imitate*—"Do as I do." Kids keep following the leader because she does things everyone in line behind her can imitate. If she does things the other kids can't—perhaps she's a gymnast and does a round off or double back flip—the game becomes "Watch the Performer" not "Follow the Leader," and the kids will soon lose interest.

That often is what happens in church. We forget that leaders are supposed to have followers. When church leaders stop doing things others can imitate, when they do ministry double back flips, is it any wonder people aren't following?

If we are doing something in ministry that we cannot train anyone else in our congregation to do, it is probably something we should stop doing. We are *performing* rather than *leading*. We hold on to certain jobs because we think we are the only ones who can do them correctly. We are not discipling people, we are defrauding them. Paul said, "Follow my example, as I follow the example of Christ" (1 Cor. 11:1). Paul knew how to play "Follow the Leader." Whatever people saw Paul doing, they could aspire to do as well.

In the early stages of a ministry, pastors may do things that others cannot, such as vision casting, preaching, and managing volunteers, but even these can eventually be training grounds for others. Not *everyone* can do *everything* we do in ministry. Not everyone can teach well in a large-group setting, but most people can learn to effectively share the Word of God in a small group. The point is that they can learn *how* we teach, not just *what* we teach. That is a process in their lives, since most people are not born teachers. Not only can most people in our church group learn to do their own limited imitation of what we do in ministry, but individuals within the church can do the specific things we do as well as, if not better than, we can do them! If we can administrate the volunteer corps of the church, then someone else in the church can too.

Finding that administratively gifted person and developing him or her will take a period of time, but if we believe that there is someone, we will find that person much more surely than if we don't believe it. A prospector *looking for* gold is more likely to *discover* it. Though the California Gold Rush started by accident when a man stumbled upon some nuggets, accidental discovery was not the primary prospecting method employed by the "forty-niners."

In later chapters we will look at some of the more specialized duties of the primary leader in any church group and see that those jobs should not be turned over to anyone else. The irony is that most pastors concentrate on doing the very things they ought to delegate to other people, and by leading in arenas where others could do the leading, pastors neglect to lead where only they should do the leading.

Another reason children like to play "Follow the Leader " is that they know they will get a chance to be the leader sooner or later. They endure the crazy antics of other leaders because they are looking forward to their chance and are planning ahead: *When I'm a leader, I want to spin everyone around, hop three times on my left foot, and fall to the ground.* If a girl said to her friends, "Let's play follow the leader, but there's one rule: I will always be the leader," few kids would join the game. Similarly, effective church leaders communicate the possibility of leadership to their congregation. Instead of making leaders seem like another class of human beings, the process of leadership makes other people feel that leading is something they could do too.

After one Sunday service, a woman hurriedly approached me and blurted out, "Your message changed my life!" People don't say that to me every week, so I wondered what pearl of wisdom had been in my sermon. "You said in your teaching," she continued, "that you're just a 'jerk,' but you keep moving." *I said that?* I thought. *That changed your life?* "I always thought I had to be perfect," she said. "If I couldn't get everything right, I couldn't minister. But since you're a 'jerk,' and you keep serving God, I guess I can too."

She wasn't saying this disrespectfully. I had referred to the fact that I often found myself at a loss, and I often blundered in life and in ministry. But by grace, I just keep moving ahead as best I can. The idea that ministry is carried on by imperfect people was a revelation to her. Pastors and leaders who strain to do, with near perfection, what no one else can possibly imitate, unintentionally raise a hurdle over which the people in their church can't jump. People watch the pastoral performance and think, *There is no hope for me. I won't even try to do what the pastor does.*

Second, *leadership is not a titled position*. Leadership is not about power or control, the divine right of kings and pastors. I call this "caveman leadership": "Ugh, me leader; you do what I say." Being a leader is not telling people that they have to do everything you tell them to do.

Sometime ago I had the opportunity to speak in a church in Scandinavia, and at one service my attention was drawn to the wife of my translator. She sat off to the side with their baby, and her manner suggested that she had been traumatized. I sensed great insecurity—the kind that comes from some covenant violation in family upbringing. From my pastoral experience I knew that she would be very suspicious of anyone in authority, yet she would also want to be acknowledged by such authority. I wanted to use my stature as the guest speaker to affirm her.

I never got the chance to meet this woman in church, so afterward as she and my translator were preparing to leave, I hurried up to their car and introduced myself to her. Not really knowing what to say, I commented on their cute baby, fumbled with small talk for a while, and said good-bye. My goal was simply to register with her that I was aware of her.

Later, after the evening service, my translator asked if I could help him with a problem. As a fledgling minister, he said he felt a need for an official title in the pioneer church he was helping to start. Though he was not the pastor, he felt that his role as a volunteer would be enhanced in the eyes of the people by an official title, and he wanted me to lobby for such a designation with his pastor. "If I had a title," he said, "the people would respect me more, and I'd have more of a platform to speak into their lives."

"A title won't help you," I responded. Feeling freedom to speak forthrightly to him, I continued, "You don't understand what true ministry is all about. Real ministry is more about what you do behind the scenes when nobody knows you are doing it. The public activity is legitimized by what we do off the platform. Let's take your wife, for instance. Has your platform ministry done much to patch her up? I don't think so. Your wife is hurting, isn't she?"

His body language said, *You would have to bring her up*.

"Do you know why I spent so much energy to get over to your car this afternoon to say hello to your wife? She has been hurt. I don't know how. I wanted her to know she is a person in her own right, that she was noticed, and that God cares about her. That's what ministry is all about. Real authority reaches into people's lives to assure them of God's kindness and goodness. If you learn to minister better without a platform, then you'll know better how to minister with the platform that God will give you."

This man received my advice well, and since then I have learned that both his marriage and his ministry are doing much better.

Third, *leadership is not a personality trait*. The prevailing literature on leadership tries to identify the characteristics of effective leaders in an effort to dissect leadership down to its component parts. Though I do not totally disagree with looking at effective leaders as role models, I do not think that trait analysis tells the most important part of the story. Leadership isn't something we *have*, like some sort of material possession. Leaders aren't supposed to become clones of some famous leader, having the same personality traits. Different people suit different needs. In any given scenario different personalities can lead effectively.

For example, the woman who was once in charge of women's ministries at our church was a prophetic sort, strong in prayer and gifted at drawing Old Testament parallels to women's situations. Her strong personality was a magnet that attracted women to seek her counsel. Our next leader didn't have the same Old Testament prophetic sense about her, but she offered stable leadership that inspired confidence, and she was an incredible mobilizer, a person who could talk to anyone and make him or her feel comfortable, included, and significant. Her gifting was that of a discerning teacher. As a result, our women's ministries changed. Instead of having one key leader, many women were mobilized. Personality is not the key issue in leadership.

Fourth, *leadership is not control*. Consider two pictures representing vastly different concepts of leadership. The first image is a commander in charge of riot police whose orders are to keep an unruly crowd from getting out of hand. In this concept of leadership, the most important thing is to be in charge, to keep people under control. The second image is the trail boss on a wagon train. In this case, leadership means finding a way to get a group of people from one place to another.

The process we want for our leadership is the process of *taking* our people somewhere, not *keeping* them somewhere. Church leadership is not about control but about movement, as we saw in the river and lake analogies. We are called to *move* people toward the will of God. The people in our charge follow because they want to reach the destination to which the Lord is calling them. Moving people toward ever-greater significance and responsibility in the Lord is the best way to keep them focused: "Where there is no vision, the people are unrestrained" (Prov. 29:18 NASB). Pointing them toward a future sight keeps them from scattering in chaos.

Each year our church conducts a summer vacation Bible school program for one week from 9:00 A.M. to 5:00 P.M. Approximately four hundred first through fifth graders participate, along with nearly two hundred adult volunteers. As wonderful as that may sound, the really incredible fact is that we mobilize about sixty middle-school kids to help our adult team leaders. We call them "counselors-in-training." Instead of having the discipline problems that one would expect with such a mob of that age group, we have a great group of helpers who are close enough in age to relate to the elementary school kids we are targeting with our VBS. We are leading them in leadership and are building in them an expectation for their future.

CULTIVATING CREDIBILITY

The primary activity of the leadership process is to cultivate influence in people's lives by building credibility with them through the context of relationship. People want to know the one whom they are following. A pastor cannot be good friends with everyone in the church, but through personal illustrations in sermons, counseling experiences, and times of fellowship, people come to feel that they know their pastor. A pastor who is known will have more influence than a pastor who remains aloof from the congregation.

A relationship is the sum of what we have learned about a person and how what we know makes us feel toward that person. That is why we introduce guest speakers by giving the people in our church some background about the speaker that will encourage them to open up to what the speaker will be saying. Imagine how much more relational context the people in our churches need with us before they will open the deep issues of their souls to us. By regularly sharing personal anecdotes in our sermons, we can acknowledge our humanity, and at the same time we will become real people, rather than just symbols, in the eyes of our congregants.

Because of past hurts and disappointments, people associate many strange thoughts, unrealistic expectations, and fears with authority *figures*. The only way to overcome those false expectations and fears is to be genuinely ourselves. We are not our position; neither are we what others have associated with people in our position. We are simply people like them—people who have been granted an extraordinary privilege of providing an example for others to follow. That example must be realistic and plausible or it will not be credible in their eyes. We must be people of credibility as well as of integrity.

Spiritual integrity is something we have because of what we do and say *in the eyes of God,* "who tests our hearts" (1 Thess. 2:4).

It is what keeps us from becoming people-pleasers and self-servers. Integrity shows itself mostly in private when no one is around. *Spiritual credibility*, on the other hand, comes as a result of what we do and say *in the eyes of people* when we engage in "doing what is good" and accomplishing things that are "excellent and profitable for everyone" (Titus 3:8). When our relationship with God meaningfully impacts our relationships with others, we develop credibility. Just as "Jesus grew in wisdom and stature, and in favor with God and men" (Luke 2:52), so, too, must spiritual leaders increase in both integrity and credibility.

Not only does credibility develop within the context of relationships, but it exists only as long as the pastor and people share a common purpose or vision. No matter how much a leader is respected, that leader loses credibility the moment people perceive that the leader is at cross-purposes with them. When people doubt that their pastor has the same goals in mind as they do, they will begin to resist the pastor's influence and credibility.

Thus, this is one of the trickiest aspects of spiritual leadership. We must teach people truth that challenges their choices in life, yet our influence wanes when they don't like the direction we are taking them. Many church splits are a result of lost influence—people deciding the pastor doesn't know what he is doing *because* he is introducing contemporary worship, moving toward a cell-group structure, hiring a youth pastor, planning to enlarge the sanctuary, and so on. How do we navigate the tension between going where we feel led by God and maintaining our leadership credibility in the lives of people who don't necessarily want to go there?

Moses suffered that tension. Time and again, the people who were being led out of slavery and into promise grumbled and complained about his leadership—where he was taking them and how he was doing it. He was challenged by his associate pastors (Aaron and Miriam) as well as the elders. While he was up on the mountain, the leaders chose a new captain who would taken them where they wanted to go.

That can happen to us. While we are receiving counsel and direction from the Lord for our people, they can be in the midst of *planning* their own way. They will want to dismiss us in favor of the new leadership because they do not want to go where we are led to take them.

THE REAL QUESTION

The real question of leadership doesn't come up until this crunch point is reached. As long as the leader is going where the followers want the leader to go, it is impossible to tell how good the leader is. The leader's credibility might be a result of nothing more than not bucking the system. Many pastors have "no problems" in their churches simply because they refuse to take the people anywhere the people don't want to go. They are not good leaders; they're just peacekeepers.

We see this in the story of Aaron's assuming leadership over the people of Israel when they perceived that Moses was taking too long in coming down from the mountain. In effect, disgruntled followers decided that Moses was no longer a credible leader, and they asked Aaron to lead them where they wanted to go. They wanted to follow a god who would do their bidding, so they needed a leader who would do the same. Though commissioned by the people, Aaron was not the leader that Moses was. Aaron's leadership let the people "get out of control" (Ex. 32:25)—he left them exposed and vulnerable to deception because he let them do what they wanted to do. Godly leaders have to balance credibility and integrity *in the eyes of people* with the same *in the eyes of God*.

FOR THE FUTURE

True leadership is cultivating in people today such influence and credibility that they will be willing to follow a course they would not otherwise choose for themselves in the future. Leadership is a process of cultivating future influence in people. That influence increases over time with each successive and positive impact on another's life. We earn credibility one small step at a time. We lead by degree, not decree.

Our leadership quotient is the sum of all our positive input into others' lives, which gives them courage to follow us into something new for the sake of accomplishing something great. If our most recent counsel for their work situation or their marriage went bust, they will be less inclined to follow our counsel next time. On the other hand, when our sermons leave them thinking, *This guy must be reading my mail*, they feel we're tracking with them, and it builds their confidence in us.

Credibility is based on a meaningful track record with people: remembering the name of their neighbor who asked for prayer last week, following up a conversation we had last month with a question of concern, touching their arm and smiling when we pass them in the foyer, taking forty seconds to alert them to a verse God put on our hearts for them, and so on. A leader can build credibility only a little bit at a time. It is not a one-time performance. It is a lifestyle, a process that goes somewhere like a river.

The incremental growth of credibility explains why pastors must serve four to seven years before they can truly lead a congregation. When I set off to plant The Coastlands, my pastor gave me some advice that, at the time, I thought was odd. "Remember," he said, "you won't have been there for years until you've been there for years."

Thank you for that spiritual tidbit, I thought. *What am I supposed to do with that?* Over time, however, I realized the meaning of what he said. There are no shortcuts in the process of gaining influence with others. The love and trust I had with the people in our church in Los Angeles did not transfer to the people I was meeting and trying to lead in Santa Cruz.

My experience with the people whom I had been pastoring for several years left me unprepared for what I experienced with the people whom I was just starting to pastor. I was surprised and a bit shocked at their suspicion toward me as a pastor. For a while I fell into the temptation of being personally wounded by their doubts about me. I am thankful that the Lord reminded me that leadership is a process.

I had just begun the process, and the burden of proof had to be mine. I realized that these people had come from previous experiences with pastors, just as I had come from previous experiences with pastoring. If they were wrong for judging me by their past experience, then I was equally wrong for doing the same. I could not expect them to have the same trust in me that my previous flock had developed over the years. I had to start the process all over again. I determined to become their leader—not by raising my voice in command but by living among them as a real person.

THE PROCESS OF CREDIBILITY

The four key factors in the gradual cultivation of credibility are caring about people, trusting people, being a resource to people, and being vulnerable to people.

Caring about people. When others sense that we sincerely care about them and their welfare, they see us as credible and trustworthy. Too often pastors become so consumed with fulfilling their vision that they lose sight of their own people. I have fallen into that trap too many times, so I am especially alert to anything that puts the honest needs of real people in a subordinate position to the needs of our church program or structure.

At a leaders' meeting, one of our pastors suggested a way to improve our scheduling. We have a men's meeting once a month on a Saturday morning as well as a leadership meeting once a month on a Sunday night, and we always put them on the same weekend. The pastor said, "Let's move the men's meeting to another weekend, so when a person is out of town, he won't have to miss both the leaders' meeting and the men's meeting."

"How we schedule this probably doesn't matter that much," I responded. "What's important is what motivates our decision. There are pluses and minuses for each way of scheduling. There isn't a right and a wrong way of scheduling the meetings, as long as we communicate to the people that we are doing it for their sake. All most people need to hear is that they are being thought of." If we keep both meetings on the same weekend, we free up three other weekends for them each month; if we put the meetings in different weeks, we make it less likely that they will have to miss both.

Although we left the schedule as it was, I thanked the pastor for his sensitivity to people, and I communicated the conversation with our church as an example of the sort of thing to which we wanted to remain alert.

When people sense that leaders' decisions about policy and programs reflect a heartfelt concern for their welfare, credibility climbs. Caring is usually communicated by small things. People sense we care when we ask about the health of the aunt for whom they asked us to pray three months ago. Caring means remembering names. "I'm not good at remembering names," you may say. My advice to all leaders is to become good at it. People carry their names for a lifetime; they're important to them. If we do not demonstrate enough care to remember people's names, why would they possibly imagine that we care about their issues?

Trusting people. Another way we build credibility is by demonstrating trust in others. People distrust those who distrust them. If you're suspicious of me, it makes me suspicious of you. If you suggest I have a hidden agenda, I think, *What's with this hidden agenda stuff? You're probably the one with the hidden agenda.*

Jesus explained this principle of reciprocity when he said, "Do to others what you would have them do to you" (Matt. 7:12). Not only is this a command, but it is sound advice for leaders who want to develop credibility. What we do to or for others will usually lead them to do the same. We can affect their future behavior by our current doings. Leaders are models, not commanders. Jesus asked us to follow his example. Leaders ask the same thing.

At The Coastlands, we have several work parties to fix up the old convent we lease. At work parties, I come and work, but I intentionally decline any position of authority. I'm just a grunt who's pretty good with a shovel or chain saw. Of course new people don't catch on right away, and they will come and ask me how I want something done.

"I don't know," I reply. "Better ask somebody who's in charge."

I am showing people that I trust the leaders we have put in charge of the work. I don't second-guess them. When I say to a carpenter, "I'm here to carry wood for you or whatever you need. Just tell me what to do," it unnerves them at first. Then they get into it. You can see them light up when they sense that I really do trust them to do what's right. And it's fun for them to have a chance to tell the pastor what to do and where to go.

People aren't dumb. Pastors and church leaders would do well to consider the trust issue from the people's perspective. Imagine dealing with a pastor who didn't trust you to oversee the

Christmas banquet or plan an outreach, but he expected you to trust him with your soul. What pastors think of people is probably a fair measure for what people ought to think of them in return. Leaders set the trust level. Trust may be risky because people do sometimes fail us, but ultimately trust is powerful.

Being a resource to people. The more we are a resource to people on organizational, theological, family, financial, and spiritual life issues, the more credibility we will come to have with them. To be a resource means that we supply people with support, aid, counsel, direction, comfort, understanding, insight, and so on. It means that we make such things available to them, not necessarily all by ourselves, but by linking them to others who can provide what they need. Being resourceful involves the capacity for dealing with tough situations or for meeting difficulties.

Leadership is like the standing offer I have with my wife: If she cannot open a jar, I am her first resource. Hopefully, I can help. Normally, people seek help only when they cannot do something themselves. Leaders must be ready to help. Though I have a deep fear that my wife will ask me to open a jar that I am too weak to open (macho flak), I cannot afford to refuse her request if I want to be asked in the future. Not being able to open a jar (it hasn't happened yet) is not the same as not being willing to try.

I have about an eighteen-month battle plan with new attenders. I begin by being a resource to them about nonpersonal needs such as information regarding the church. Most new people want to understand what is going on, so after they have attended for a few weeks, I'll ask simple questions such as, "What do you think about our church?" and "How is it different from other churches you have attended?" After I have helped orient them to our church and have explained things like why we raise our hands in worship or why we have cell groups, they feel more confident to test me as a resource on more sensitive issues, such as whether they must forgive someone who hasn't asked for forgiveness.

Usually when people ask a theological question or when they want me to explain some verse in the Bible, they are waiting to see to what extent my words relate to their own life-situation. People are not very interested in theology. They don't relate well to it. They are interested in knowing if that theology relates to them. I try to explain what things mean by using examples from my own life or from other real-life situations. For example, a man recently asked me about submission. He had probably been bruised by some authority figure in his life, and he was almost daring me to tell him what it would mean for him to submit to leaders in the church. He wasn't really wanting to debate. He just wanted to know if he would be safe at our church. Having observed enough of his dealings with his wife and children, I went after an example to which he could relate.

"I try to remember," I began, "that the word *submit* is used both in family and church contexts. Therefore, whatever it means that a wife should do in reference to her husband, is the same as he should do in reference to his spiritual leaders."

As is usually the case in the lives of people who ask such questions, the man had two definitions in mind—one for a wife to her husband and one for himself to his pastor. He was careful with his wife; leaders had not been careful with him. Debating and defining submission would not really help.

A lady came up to me after the service a couple of months ago, and she wanted to know if my sermon was talking about the same thing as a verse she had just read the night before in her devotions. She was obviously excited at the prospect that God had clued her in on the message before he delivered it to the whole church. I could tell it meant so much to her because of her struggle with feelings of unworthiness.

Her real question was not about content, although I did confirm that her verse and my sermon text were both talking about the future blessings God promises to us. Her real questions were, "Is it possible that God spoke to me, and that I really heard him?" and "Will this ever happen to me again?"

I said, "That's what happens when we read. Sometimes the Lord speaks to us. And to let us know it really is he, he confirms his words with other people and situations. You are right on track. Thank you for being a confirmation to me. I needed that encouragement."

Being vulnerable to people. People distrust someone who seems to be hiding things, and they trust someone who is open and vulnerable. I have found that my credibility increases as I am willing to disclose who I am, in my sermons. This doesn't mean preaching an elaborate theology of me: "Let's turn in the text of my heart to. . . ." Rather, when I illustrate, I often try to disclose something of who I am so that people feel they know me—and that I am still growing and being corrected by the Lord.

In one sermon I tried to get a little humor out of the idea that, as a church, we don't like to use the word *committed*. My impression through the years is that leaders use the word *committed* as a way of getting people to come to events that may not be that good in the first place. When I was in college, leading Bible studies that invariably fell off in attendance as the quarter progressed, I tried my hand at "getting people more committed." I was going to have them sign a "commitment covenant" promising to attend the Bible study every week. My wife, Pamela, made an off-hand remark that has shaped much of my thinking since: "It seems to me," she breezed, "that people go to things that really help them. If they aren't coming, maybe it isn't that useful to them." So, I told the congregation that we don't use the word *committed*:

"Committed is something you are to an institution—like an asylum or a prison."

While people were laughing at my wit, I felt the hand of God whack me a good one on my backside. *Whoa, what was that for?* I wondered. I kept preaching, but I knew I had somehow displeased God. Then I realized there likely were people in the congregation who themselves had been through the sadness and horror of being institutionalized—for whatever reasons. For people who have suffered severe psychospiritual disorders or who have paid for crimes in prison, it was no joke. For the sake of a little humor, I had unintentionally brought shame and agony to their hearts.

I debated whether to stop everything and apologize or wait till the end of the sermon. Finally I decided, when in doubt, 'fess up. "Excuse me," I said; "these sermon points are important, but nowhere near as important as what just happened to me. I want to ask your forgiveness for the unkind remark I made."

I referred to my bad pun and said, "I tried harder to be funny than to be sensitive. It was cheap. I've just felt God's displeasure at what I said, and so I want to ask your forgiveness and the Lord's forgiveness."

No one remembers the sermon from that day. But no one has forgotten the lesson.

Vulnerability also means acknowledging my weaknesses. Secular researchers have done a host of studies to determine what the average person wants most in a leader. The top two desired traits are no surprise: honesty and competence. But being competent doesn't mean trying to do everything. In fact, I have discovered that when I acknowledge my weaknesses, people assume I must be competent in other things. It's a reverse psychology that flies in the face of the traditional assumption that a leader gains credibility by appearing superhuman. People don't trust superhumans, though, because they have seen that superhumans tend to fall. Acknowledge your weaknesses; when possible, hire staff to handle areas of your weaknesses; or get volunteers to compensate for them. But don't try to cover them up. Clay feet are too bulky to hide.

People will not usually follow a leader who doesn't have true authority in their eyes. If we don't have authority, we don't have leadership—period. When we have true authority, everything else flows from it. Our congregation will decide whether or not to follow us in a new direction primarily as a result of what they think about us—weighing the relative discomfort they feel about the new direction we are leading them in against the comfort they have previously experienced under our care.

Leadership is not something we do only in front of a crowd of people. It is too bad that *leadership*, like *discipleship*, is a static-state noun in our language. The real heart of the biblical concept would be better translated *leadering*—a process of being and doing for others.

Chapter Three

COMMUNICATING VISION

A pastor who has spent the last nine years faithfully serving the same group of people in his church might well ask, "If leadership is all about developing a meaningful track record with people—of servanthood and 'being there for them'—then why haven't I been able to do more with my church? What am I supposed to be able to do with my leadership quotient once I have it?"

Though some pastors never get around to asking this question, effective church leaders recognize that there must be more of a reason for having church than merely having church. Church cannot be an end in and of itself. It must be a means to some other end. Is it a vehicle to take people somewhere, or is it the destination itself? We can better understand this issue by picturing a block of marble ready to be sculpted and a chisel in the hand of a sculptor. You as pastor are the sculptor. Is the chisel in your hand the church ready to chip away at the people, or do you see the people as the chisel you use to shape the church?

Proving to people that our authority is intended solely for their benefit—not our own—is just the beginning for the process of church leadership. Leadership is a highly specialized role that goes beyond the kinds of things our compassionate hearts naturally know to do. There is a great deal more to being an effective church leader than demonstrating concern and spiritual insight. Not recognizing the sorts of leadership skills we will be discussing in the following chapters, many godly, caring, and spiritual saints struggle in their role as the primary leader of their church or ministry group.

A few years ago, Michael Gerber exploded one of America's most cherished notions about business entrepreneurs in a book entitled *The E-Myth*.[1] Gerber contends that most new companies and commercial ventures are not started by pioneer-spirited risk-takers who plunge ahead boldly, but by people who "in a moment of idiocy" think to themselves, *I shouldn't be working for someone else. I ought to start my own business and make all this money for myself.*

A carpenter who pounds nails for journeyman's wages begins to calculate, with each swing of the hammer, what he could make if he ran his own contracting business. Finally he takes the plunge. Before long, his desk overflows with invoices, tax records, receipts, and estimates. He cannot understand why he loses employees in less than six months. He doesn't know how to budget the company's funds, and suppliers hound him for payment on overdue bills. He works more hours per week than he expected, many of them consumed by bidding new jobs and trying to calculate workmen's compensation payments. He discovers that though he was a skilled carpenter, he is not a businessman. After two years, he decides that contracting is too big a hassle and closes his business.

The problem with such entrepreneurs, says Gerber, is not what seems obvious—for example, that the skills needed for running a software production company differ from the skills needed to design software. The lack of overlap between work skills and overall leadership skills is a huge hurdle. What makes it insurmountable is that most entrepreneurs do not realize their need to acquire a different set of skills soon enough.

Like the E-Myth for entrepreneurs, there is an M-Myth for ministers. Many pastors go into full-time ministry with the same motives I had. I was happily minding my own business as a college student and later as a college instructor, but I became increasingly addicted to the delight of teaching the Word of God, praying for and counseling people, and helping them discover who and what they were meant to be in God. I decided that full-time, vocational ministry was the way to fulfill this insatiable yearning to touch people with the love of God.

Once in pastoral ministry, however, I discovered the truth. If I really wanted freedom to minister to people, I ought to quit pastoring and go back to my old job! I was buried under an avalanche of *ad-ministry*, working hard each day to clean my desk so I could finally get my hands on somebody to whom I could minister.

There is a vast difference between personal ministry skills—counseling people, teaching the Bible, praying for people—and leadership skills. We assume that since we have been sheep, we can be shepherds. Munching on the grass is one thing, but it's quite another to be the person who watches for wolves and plans which field to take the flock to next.

When we fail to realize that the skills an individual needs to bring the life of Christ to others bear little resemblance to the skills pastors need to mobilize a congregation, we end up frustrated. We grow frustrated, because no matter how diligently we teach and counsel and pray one-on-one, our congregation as a whole still seems stymied. And so are we. We work harder at the ministry skills that served us so well in the past with people, but the church as an organization doesn't seem to improve.

That is where specific leadership skills come in. No leadership or training is meant to substitute for personal ministry skills or personal devotion to the Lord. We aren't to sacrifice integrity for gimmickry or to surrender our call to follow hard after the Lord by taking some organizational shortcut to corporate ministry effectiveness. The Bible instructs individual believers in how to live and minister, but it also has specific counsel for leaders (for example, "Be shepherds of God's flock that is under your care, . . . not because you must, but because you are willing . . .; not lording it over those entrusted to you, but being examples to the flock" [1 Peter 5:2–3]; "Not many of you should presume to be teachers, my brothers, because you know that we who teach will be judged more strictly" [James 3:1]). As surely as the Scriptures distinguish the qualifications of leaders and their responsibilities from what is asked of new converts, so, too, ought pastors to recognize that there are organic as well as spiritual differences between being a member of a church and being the leader of it.

THE COMPELLING FORCE OF VISION

The most critical and foundational skill pastors need for leading their whole flock is *communicating vision*. Both words are important. First we must have a vision, but we also must be able to communicate that vision compellingly. Vision can best be understood as the essential calling for the congregation—knowing God's basic design and purpose for it as a whole. Vision answers the dual questions: Why does this church exist? and What is it supposed to do in the years ahead? Vision always speaks about the desired future of an organization, so pastors must formulate and communicate a forward-looking declaration of what their churches are all about—and why.

Vision is the central dynamic of any leader's responsibility. Peter Drucker, who is acknowledged as the leading thinker on non-profit organizations, puts vision's importance this way: "What matters is not the leader's charisma. What matters is the leader's mission. Therefore the first job of the leader is to think through and define the mission of the institution."[2] Joe Ellis writes in *The Church on Purpose,* "Power and growth depend on the ability to mobilize the people around a well-defined, central purpose"—a high sense of mission—a spiritual mandate, a God-given objective.[3]

People want a mission, to be part of something compelling and meaningful. About three years ago I had a real need for someone to lead and undertake the development of two particular ministries in our church, but little money was available for salaries. Two single women in our church, both in their mid-thirties, had deep commitments to these respective ministry arenas. Believing that our need was part of fulfilling our vision and not just a nice idea, I approached one of the women about becoming the resident director of our internship training program by saying, "I've sensed you believe in training people for ministry. I want you to pray about coming on staff full-time to develop our intern program into something that will impact the world. We can only pay you $650 a month plus room and board." It took her barely a day to make a dramatic career decision: she signed on with us.

I made roughly the same offer to the other woman to head our ministry to college students. She, too, jumped at the opportunity to sacrifice her career for the sake of the work of Christ. The vision, and my commitment to it, gave me the courage to ask these women to leave their vocational and financial security to do something incredible for the Lord. Their belief in and commitment to the vision inspired them to make the sacrifice.

Wherever you see a church with a host of committed and sacrificial workers, volunteer or paid, you can be sure a leader has communicated a compelling vision. Our job as pastors is to conceive and communicate our church's mission in such a way that others are inspired to give their lives away to fulfill it.

Clear vision enables others to see their place in the picture. They can see how their gifts and passions relate to what God is calling their church to do. Our mission enables us to legitimately invite others to help. It shows that we are not just inviting people to help make our church big and ourselves famous. It answers their question about why God has placed them in a certain church at a particular point in time.

At each of our membership interest meetings, we use the illustration of a large woven basket that God is shaping, one strand at a time. Though we don't yet know the new people at those meetings well, we want them to know that we presume God has a reason for asking them to partner with us at this point in our church's life. Their uniqueness and personal calling in the Lord will help us to fulfill our vision, just as we intend for our church's calling to further them in their ministry development. Linking our mission with their gifting—when offered, not imposed upon—increases their sense of involvement and significance.

Discussion about mission statements and distinctive visions for church can be disturbing to leaders who somehow imagine that all churches have the same mission: "Other than doctrine and polity, don't (shouldn't) all churches do the same thing?" Some pastors balk at defining visions for their churches that are any more specific than the church's ultimate assignment to fulfill the Great Commission and glorify God. Shouldn't every church have the same vision?

Ultimately, yes, but in the specifics, no. One local congregation cannot be the entire body of Christ. Just as there are many individual parts of the human body—eyes, feet, ears—and there are various ministry giftings—teachers, pastors, evangelists—so there are unique congregational assignments and ministry orientations. Though each individual believer lives most of his or her spiritual life according to perspectives and patterns that are common to all the saints of God, such as loving one's neighbors and praying, some assignments and callings are unique, such as Moses' commission at the burning bush and Paul's call to take the gospel to the Gentiles.

Though possessed of the same faith, believers in God conquered kingdoms, administered justice, shut the mouths of lions, and routed foreign armies (Heb. 11:33–34). They did not all do the same things even though they believed in the same God. God has prepared good works for each believer to walk in. The same holds true for churches, as we can see by reading Christ's letters to the seven churches in Revelation 2–3.

To cast a compelling vision, a pastor or leader must be comfortable with each church having differences that complement the God-given, unique assignments of other churches. Unity of purpose is not the same as conformity of mission. Each believer and each congregation has a unique and specialized role to play just as on a football team each player has a specific assignment. A player helps the team most if he pays complete attention to his assignment and doesn't overzealously try to do everyone else's job. A defensive end who chases a play too far from his assigned area breaks containment, and if the ball carrier goes back to the space the lineman vacated, the play will lead to a big gain for the other team. One player cannot be the entire football team, and one church cannot reach an entire city, much less a nation or the world. Each church is a player on Christ's team.

If we embrace the limitations of focus and come to grips with the assignment the King has for our congregation, we become far more effective. The more generic we are, the less focused we are and ultimately the less effective. Generalities prevent us from evaluating our effectiveness and making adjustments. The less particular our mission as defined by our goals, the less likely we will be to give what we're doing a good hard look. Instead, we will content ourselves with waiting for something to happen. The people who follow us will, in turn, slip into the same mentality of waiting to see what will happen instead of stepping up to make things happen.

We must be careful to balance the "step-up" mentality so that we do not "labor in vain" trying to build something that God is not building. Jesus taught us to calculate the cost of our building projects to ensure that we have enough resources to complete them. That calculating process requires us to have a finished house in mind—that is, we have to know what we are trying to build before we can determine its cost. An effective leader envisions the completed project and shows it to all the builders so that they know where they're headed.

MOVING FROM GENERAL TO SPECIFIC

To be compelling, a vision must be stated in terms of how we will view success. What is the primary result we are trying to accomplish? It helps to ask God for specific Bible texts that capsulize your sense of calling as a church. For instance, Isaiah 61 has been especially meaningful to me and my congregation. It speaks of restoring ravaged and broken people into "oaks of righteousness" who will restore others. It gives us a backdrop for "mobilizing mended nurturers." From their earliest exposure to our church, newcomers are presented with simple statements and pictures of what our church is all about. We will spend whatever time is needed to see people recovered from the ravages of life so that they will spend whatever time is needed to help someone else recover, and so on down the line.

As mentioned above, a compelling vision must be stated both as an ultimate goal and in specific process terms. Take our vision at The Coastlands, for example. Our overarching mission is simple. We love, mend, train, and send people. Our goal is to develop people into what they might not be able to become if left to their own devices. We want to do to them so that they can do unto others. We want each of them to experience meaningful, personal development so that they will be better able to assist others in the same process.

But what exactly does that involve? What activities, programs, and processes enable us to fulfill that mission? How will we succeed and know that we have succeeded? There are two ways to approach the task of defining success. We can determine specific numeric goals (attendance, conversions, baptisms, offerings, churches pioneered, and so on) or we can envision an ideal process/environment that will most likely produce the results we want (teaching settings, activities, counseling and care networks, worship, and so on). We can have numeric goals or process goals. At The Coastlands we mostly opt for the process goals, trying to imagine the best configuration of our total resources.

The day after Christmas in 1984, when my wife, Pamela, and I moved from Los Angeles to Aptos with a few people to pioneer The Coastlands, I had a dream in my heart of six church process elements that would give us an excellent opportunity to fulfill our mission. I offer these to you not as a prototype of what *every* church ought to have but simply as a specific example of the kind of vision-driven components an effective leader must spell out for the people to link up with. Although I cannot guarantee that we will fulfill our mission just because we have these elements in our total configuration, I do believe that they will give us the best opportunity to do so.

Again, without authentic spiritual life born of our obedience to Jesus Christ, no church process will bear lasting fruit. Flesh and blood—no matter how sincere or thoughtful—cannot inherit the kingdom. Human reasoning and planning alone will not translate into spiritually impacting activity. But presuming genuine love for God and people, some type of purposeful arrangement of church is an essential activity for a good leader.

The development of our vision came as a consequence of asking myself a simple question: What do you want the church to have in its program, and what do you want to be doing in the future as a church? From the earliest days of our church, I have wanted to cast a vision in terms of these specifics:

1. *Cell groups that nurture people and multiply.* I wasn't interested in starting groups that were primarily oriented toward caring for one another. Caring is merely the first step in the process of nurturing and discipling people. Caring does build credibility so that we are given the opportunity to assist people's spiritual growth, but fellowship without an eye toward eventual nurture and discipleship can easily become a clique.

I wanted the groups to keep expanding and multiplying, so I was not interested in cell groups that stayed together for several years. I am not opposed to "covenant groups," I just don't feel called to have them in our church. I had two reasons for aiming at constant multiplication: a desire to reach more people and a dream to mobilize people for leadership. A set number of groups would limit the number of leaders, but multiplying groups would force new leaders to the fore. People who had never dreamed of leading a group would find themselves doing that very thing.

Isaiah 60:22 expresses our vision for leaders and groups: "The smallest one will become a clan, and the least one a mighty nation" (NASB). My hope for every willing person—sooner or later—is that he or she will become the leader of a small group and know the joy of nurturing others. The great addiction of ministry is seeing change in others. When I ask pastors why they are willing to endure the pain and heartache of ministry, they all give me the same answer: "I get to watch people change and grow in the Lord." Somehow, seeing others be transformed allows us to forget all the hassles we went through with them. My theory is quite simple: If the clergy are kept in the pulpit because they see those they serve being changed and restored, it is what will keep the layperson ministering too. Multiplying cell groups will give an increasing number of laypeople the thrill of being part of God's transforming work.

In our cell groups we aim for 110 percent involvement in our Sunday adult attendance. We are pleased to have people in cell groups even before they come to our church services. Right now 84 percent of those in (adult) services also attend cell groups. To me that is fairly successful, but we are not completely satisfied. When our cell groups invite friends from outside the church at least as much as they invite fellow churchgoers, our percentage will rise.

2. *A dynamic, contemporary, weekly celebration.* Because I knew the key to missions was to find "cultural equivalents" to the truths of the gospel and to speak in the language (culture) of the people, I wanted our church to use music and language that fit our era. I wanted our total presentation—from the colors we chose for our banners to the sound of the tapes we played before service—to feel familiar to people in their twenties, thirties, and forties. I did not want to make a *statement* against any style or presentation that other pastors have adopted, but I did want to remember that the style is only a vehicle, not the essence of the message.

The vocabulary didn't really exist in 1984, but in today's terms we would not be *seeker-driven* but, rather, *seeker-sensitive*. I have no quarrel with churches whose mission it is to weave the gospel message around people's felt needs. That kind of fishing works great! Though our calling leans a bit more toward touching wounded places in people's hearts and minds than it does toward responding to their consciously felt sense of need, I still wanted to offer the people who would attend our church, songs and words that fit their culture.

People's weeks are usually fairly rough, and they don't need somber songs to sing on the weekend. There are times when we need to be reflective and quiet in the worship we sing to the Lord, but the basic tone of our church service is upbeat and crisp, with fair amounts of humor rounding off the edges. The sermons are expository—meaning we usually work our way through entire books of the Bible one verse at a time. I let the text present the outline and the main points. I switch to topical studies with enough regularity that I can cover pressing issues with ease, but those series are not the rule of thumb. Unlike seeker-driven churches, we do not use many "how-to" titles for the sermons. I avoid as much religious language as possible, substituting images and analogies for Christian jargon. Hence, the subject matter is timeless, but the language is timely.

3. *Missions.* Because I believe our calling should extend beyond our cultural borders, I wanted to have ample opportunity for our people to travel to other lands and to receive guests from other nations. We regularly send short-term mission groups and receive teams from other parts of the world, particularly Europe. On any given day that you visit our church, you can find up to a dozen Europeans helping us and learning about ministry.

The sending and receiving of mission groups has benefited us tremendously. It breaks people from Santa Cruz out of their provincial mentality by putting them in contact with believers who think and speak differently. In addition, the teamwork developed in the months leading up to the actual mission trips our people have taken has built unity, relationship, and esprit de corps among the adults who have gone. The common experiences of adventure and servanthood have bonded church members who might not otherwise have much contact with one another.

Since 1984 we have sent more than forty-five teams overseas, and Europeans who have come here to visit and receive training have returned to Europe and planted three congregations—in Wales, Switzerland, and Germany. The constant flow of Europeans to our church for study, vacation, and relationship has given us a true appreciation for the struggles believers face elsewhere in the world. This last summer we hosted fifty-two teenagers (children of pastors) from Europe for three weeks; they stayed in homes of people in our church. "Intermix '95" will be a point of reference and discussion for hundreds in our church for years to come.

4. *A counseling and recovery ministry.* In the process of loving, mending, and training people, I foresaw that we would encounter points of deep wounding in people's lives. Since I believe that God's Word contains "everything we need for life and godliness" (2 Peter 1:3), and that through its promises we can recover from the corruption in the world, I have been determined to offer biblical counseling and spiritual ministry to broken people without resorting to psychological orientations.

The counseling we offer is not clinical counseling or long-term therapy such as is offered by certified professionals. I don't criticize that, but our calling is to have a team of counselors who explore the Scriptures and seek the heart of God for people in need, praying for and counseling them in the things of the Spirit. Our purpose is to mend the broken and torn areas in people with the healing touch of the Holy Spirit; to encourage people to repent of their sins and to forgive the sins of others against them; and to free people from demonic bondages and spiritual distortions that have kept them from the abundant life promised by Jesus.

We deal with issues from a spiritual perspective—that is, we try to see things in terms of the battle between righteousness and unrighteousness, the spirit and the flesh, the power of God and the influence of the devil; to look for the biblical principles and dynamics involved in the situations for which counsel is sought. This kind of counseling is consistent with our vision for how God wants to transform people and their situations by the power of his Word and his Spirit.

5. *An internship program*. Having entered the ranks of full-time ministry without graduating from a seminary or Bible college, I wanted to make the same jump from the secular marketplace to Christian ministry available to dedicated young people at The Coastlands. In my mind I envisioned a residential training program that would be a cross between a Bible college and a parachurch ministry training center. I had started a similar program at the church from which we were coming, and I wished to develop the concept more at our new church.

One of the nice fringe benefits of an internship program—where the interns pay the church to be trained—is that it significantly increases the church staff. Our hope is to simulate full-time church work so the interns can get a feel for what they are likely to encounter in their future ministries. We give them Mondays off, and they work like regular staff the rest of the week. Monday through Friday they have classes for one or two hours taught by one of the pastors, and every Friday I have breakfast with them. For the first several years, the interns were housed in several ways—collectively in apartments, individually in their own homes, and so on. We now lease a former convent as our church facility, so that enables us to have a residential internship program right on campus.

6. *Access groups*. Access groups are outreaches based on various interests—from playing on a baseball team to taking classes in quilting, photography, or upholstering—anything that would give our people an event to which they could invite their neighbors or friends. Since I was a college English instructor before I became a pastor, I thought it would be exciting to offer a class in which we would discuss the best novels of world literature. Such a class would provide a forum for dialogue and relationship. I thought our guests would be intrigued to discover that their professor was a preacher.

Anything that would expose me to the community and the community to me was worth looking into. Within weeks of moving to Santa Cruz, I signed up as a soccer coach for my oldest son's team. I had never played soccer in my life, but coaching gave me access to people whom I would otherwise never encounter. Ten years and seventeen teams later, I think coaching was one of the best moves I ever made. It kept me honest with my schedule, with my family priorities, and with my perspective on the lost people I was trying to reach.

Sports teams, toddlers' play groups, 50s Valentine's parties, Trivial Pursuit tournaments—we've tried all kinds of things to mingle our people with people in our community. One church I know of put on an all-day landscaping seminar. The church was located near a new housing development, and people really appreciated that the church would help them with such practical things.

We have been working on these elements since starting the church, and the access groups are the only element we have not developed fully to our satisfaction. We will keep trying new and different approaches to that component of our process; and until we do get it, we can feel fairly encouraged to remember that not everything happens overnight. That is the beauty of process thinking: we don't have to give ourselves a final grade; we can give ourselves a mid-term progress report. Our access groups have struggled, but we keep tinkering, and eventually we're going to get it right.

COMMUNICATING THE VISION

Securing the vision is only half of an effective leader's task; equally important is *communicating* the vision in a compelling manner. Even a simple vision can produce tremendous growth in an organization when the torch carrier communicates it with power. But when a leader has great ideas for ministry yet can't get the vision across, he or she is stalled in frustration.

Is communicating—being able to project the future in glowing rhetoric—an art that some people are born with? Does vision attach itself to personal charisma? Or are there basic keys to becoming a better vision-caster? What will help people grow excited about and committed to the vision God has given you for your church?

Here are seven ways to help others see what you see and feel what you feel:

Use similes and metaphors. As the word implies, vision is visual; thus, images help people picture your goals for the future.

"If you are a shiny new car," I'll say from the pulpit, "you may not want to hang out in this church, because we're like an automobile repair shop. It's likely that someone working with a wrench on the car next to you will spill grease on you or put a ding in you. If you're in such good shape that a ding will be noticed, this is not the place for you. But if you are a car that is barely running, you've come to the right place, because we specialize in working with broken cars."

In another metaphor, I recently described our church as an antique restoration factory: "In our warehouse, 90 percent of the space is taken by acid baths and refinishing areas where the antiques are stripped and then sanded and refinished. Only a small portion of floor space is for the showroom. People come in the back door, messed up as they may be, and we help restore them to their original beauty. Then we place them on display so someone else will want to come in for restoration."

Pictures are worth a thousand expository words. At almost every public service, I make some pictorial statement about how we see ourselves as a church. Sometimes the images are humorous ("We're like McGyver—we use anything to piece together your rescue"); at other times they are pointed and biblical ("Lots of people are trapped in caves with no one to bring them safely back into freedom and light. We explore caves, looking for people like you who may want to get out.").

Tell stories. Stories are the most powerful form of communication. They are easy to recall, and they convey a message more subtly than statements do. The stories we tell can come from our lives, from the lives of people in the church, from Christian and secular media—anything that illustrates our vision. We can tell stories in sermons, in the church newsletter, during announcements or worship, during a testimony time, before the offering—anytime.

We want people to feel confident that the Word of God is the most profound and life-changing Book of all. We want them to rely on it and expect to find in it all the answers they need to successfully navigate life on this planet. Therefore, I'm always on the lookout for stories that will build that confidence in people's hearts about the Bible. I don't make stories up to make a point; what I would lose by sacrificing my integrity would be greater than anything I would gain by the story's telling. One story I recently related went like this:

The other day a lady came up to me after service and blurted out, "I'm on to you. I've got you all figured out."

"Really?" I replied. "How's that?"

"I've only been coming here a few weeks. At first I thought you were so smart—that you knew all sorts of things about people and stuff."

"And . . .?"

"And now I know you aren't really that smart after all," she concluded with a triumphant grin.

My puzzled look was all the bait she needed to deliver the coup de grâce: "Now I know that you just say what is in the Bible, and everybody thinks you know so much."

"That's right," I confided with a conspiratorial look, "but don't tell anyone it's all in the Bible."

The story communicated to my congregation the truth found in Deuteronomy 4:5–6: "See, I have taught you decrees and laws as the LORD my God commanded me, so that you may follow them in the land you are entering to take possession of it. Observe them carefully, for this will show your wisdom and understanding to the nations, who will hear about all these decrees and say, 'Surely this great nation is a wise and understanding people.'"

Use teachable moments. One Sunday a young couple brought their baby for dedication. I noticed that before the mother came to the platform, she had a panicked look on her face. As the young family approached the platform, I realized why: An odorous cloud preceded them.

This is going to be interesting, I thought.

The mother had her hand clasped about the baby's leg in tourniquet fashion to stanch the flow of the odor's source. When the time came for me to take the baby in my arms to pray for her and her family, the mother gave me a look that said, *You don't want to do that.*

"I see we have had an accident," I said to the whole church. "We have a poopy baby. Well, never mind." The mother looked about ready to faint, and I took the baby in my arms. (Admittedly,

I applied my own finger-thumb tourniquet outside the mother's and held the child with legs turned away from me. No sense messing oneself up more than one has to.)

"Did you think I wouldn't take your child in my arms," I inquired, "just because he messed his pants? Don't you know that I'm used to this sort of thing. I am a father, after all ... and a pastor."

The people kept laughing even after they realized I had been speaking of them.

Then I turned to the church and exclaimed, "Isn't it great, folks, that we serve a God who never minds taking us in his arms even though we're messing our pants all the time?"

Episodes like that send the message that it's okay at our church to have problems. We don't want a church where everyone pretends that their whole lives are fine. If someone is perfectly mature, Jesus doesn't have anything to say to him or her. Jesus came to save the sickies. If people can't disclose the issues plaguing them, they have no hope of recovery. All they can do at church is become good actors. We're not a talent agency; we're a church.

Interpret circumstances. Leaders help people make sense of what's happening in the church and in their lives by interpreting events, situations, and problems in terms of the vision. "The first responsibility of a leader," says Max De Pree, former CEO of Herman Miller, "is to define reality."[4] Leaders must not use their role in a manipulative way, or to get people to see what isn't there, or to agree with them. But they can interpret circumstances so that people can see things in a good light rather than bad, for one's perspective shapes much of what one ends up seeing—a glass half full or half empty.

A few years ago we went through a period of a year and a half in our church when we lost as many as one-fourth of our people. Many were simply moving away, but a good portion didn't want to go the direction we were going in our church—toward increased servanthood and personal responsibility. Many who left had enjoyed us more as the fun church. As other people kept leaving our church, those who stayed became increasingly nervous about what was happening. Even though our total attendance never dipped—newcomers replaced those who left—I came to the place where I, too, was nervous about the exodus. But one day as I read the Bible, God helped me understand what was happening. I came across an obscure verse in the book of Leviticus that said the Israelites would "still be eating last year's harvest when [they would] have to move it out to make room for the new" (26:10). That passage enabled me to interpret our seemingly disastrous events in a positive light—that God was going to be sending us new people for the new season into which he had called us.

I shared that interpretation of Leviticus 26:1–13 with our leaders and eventually with the congregation. "I have good news for you," I said. "We are eating up the old supply to make room for the new. As these people leave (and we bless them as they go), God will bring us a new group of people." That Scripture dispelled our nervousness. Sure enough, when the year-and-a-half exodus ended, our congregation not only had maintained its average attendance but within a few months grew an additional 20 percent.

If a leader gives no interpretation of the events going on in and around the church, the people with the loudest or most persuasive voices will shape the congregation's opinions. "People can make of it what they want" is not a good credo for leaders. Our assignment is to lead—to take people where they might not get on their own. That means helping them think through the events around them.

Model the vision. Leaders must live the vision, modeling it for others to see. At The Coastlands our vision is to help wrecked people recover, so it is important that we maintain an accepting and merciful atmosphere around the church, as well as one of confession, vulnerability, and accountability. I know this will never happen unless I lead the way. The openness in our church, therefore, begins in our weekly pastors' meeting, when we devote the first hour to personal disclosure of our struggles. It's the time of week we hate—but love. By confessing our faults to one another and acknowledging our sins, we create a place of vulnerability _and_ safety. Many people fear confession because they see it involving only gross sins, such as sexual immorality, but the reason gross offenses occur is that people don't confess the little things along the way.

One week I was beset with a lingering sadness. I knew I needed to disclose this to my pastoral team. As I prayed about what could be causing this sadness, I realized it came from an attitude of "Oh, what's the difference anyway?" I felt defeated, like a basketball fan whose team is down twelve points with thirty seconds to go on the clock and the star forward fouled out. No specific problems in church had weighed especially heavy upon me, but I had somehow fallen prey to a lack of kindness toward a specific ministry group that had not been interested in my offer of help.

I acknowledged this to my fellow pastors and told them I was throwing myself back into whatever God had for me—including rejection or neglect from this ministry group. That confession saved me from a chronic, low-grade depression and, equally important, continued the process of setting a tone of openness for our church. During that time of confession and subsequent opportunities to share with individuals and with the congregation, I explained some of what God taught me about my plight: some depressions—not all—are like a warning light on the instrument panel in our cars, telling us that it is time for servicing. The car isn't about to break down, but it should be checked out soon.

God made us to work a certain way, and when we are not running properly, little signals go off. God made me to be a person with lots of faith and optimism, so if I try to live with an attitude of "What's the use?" I am not functioning normally. My depression—not everyone's—was a response to my wrongly chosen attitude toward the ministry group more than it was a response to my life's circumstances.

As I later confessed to the congregation, the episode modeled several critical values in our overall vision. First, it communicated that everyone has issues, including the pastor. Second, it showed everyone the value of confession and how much God can show us when we do acknowledge our sins. Third, it spoke of the uniqueness of each of us and how God has designed us to function.

Use repetition and variety. Preaching one sermon a year on your vision or hanging up a vision statement in the church foyer will not begin to sink the vision into people's hearts. They need to see and hear your vision dozens of times through a multitude of channels over an extended time before it will affect them. If we keep plucking the same string in the same way, people will eventually tire of it and tune us out. In most of our services, people hear me say once or twice what our mission is, but I say it differently each time. Instead of always saying that we love, mend, train, and send, I rephrase it—for example, "We want to do to you, so you can do to others. We want to help you become all God wants you to be so you can help others become what God wants them to be."

Make it personal. One of the young men in our church was thinking about pioneering a church, and like most pioneers, his feet were getting a little cold as his departure date neared. As we talked about this one day, he strayed from the topic and reported that his father who lived in another part of the country had recently come to know Jesus and had found a good church near his home.

The young man talked some more about the church planting idea until I suddenly said, "I don't want you to plant a church."

He got a puzzled look on his face. "You don't?"

"No," I said. "I want you to go and establish a congregation for someone else's dad who is going to find Jesus."

He thought for a moment, got a big grin on his face, and he hasn't looked back since. He took a team of ten adults from California to Colorado nearly two years ago, and they have a growing congregation filled with people's relatives.

When we personalize the vision for individuals, they see the application of our vision in a way they never have before.

THE CLASH OF VISION

When a leader casts a vision, two things happen. First, people who don't have a vision of their own are happy to buy into someone else's. Vision captures a crowd. The phrase _casting a vision_ is based on the image of casting a net. Second, people who have a different vision will be alerted that now is the time to find another place to go (or some choose to stay and fight for their vision). Without an agreed-upon vision, two cannot walk together. We know this from the truth of two verses of Scripture: "Where there is no vision, the people are unrestrained" (Prov. 29:18); and "Do two ever walk together unless they make an agreement?" (Amos 3:3).

Is the pastor the only person who can determine God's purpose for a church? What do you do when there are two or more different ideas for the vision put forward by the congregation? I don't believe in a heavy authoritarian sort of leadership, but from the beginning of our church, I have had a sense of our mission. People who agree with that mission have tended to stick around, and people who had another mission in mind have eventually gone elsewhere. When a new pastor moves into an established congregation, he or she doesn't face the same dynamic as the pioneer pastor of a new congregation.

I give as much freedom as possible to people so that within the confines of the larger vision, they can pursue their own. We see ourselves not merely as a large river with a lot of tributaries flowing in, but as a river flowing into a delta. My dream is to equip people to spill over the banks of this river, to spread into land that needs water and refreshment. We empower people to pursue their own vision. Nevertheless, I am not for chaos. The Bible says everything should be done decently and in order. A church can't have umpteen leaders each trying to cast a vision for the whole church.

To illustrate, when my family takes a vacation, my children go wherever I take them. That's part of being a family. Our vacations are usually great, but sometimes they're a bust because Dad came up with a bad idea. I often ask the kids where they want to go for the vacation, but the ultimate decision is mine and my wife's, and the kids go along for the ride. In churches, most people are happy to go along if our destination has significance. Eventually the relationship your people have with you and your vision coalesces, making it easy for you to lead in the future.

As we have seen, leadership is a highly specialized role in any organization. One critical task is casting vision. The ability to conceive and communicate vision and to gather a group of followers who have owned it is one of the key measures of the effectiveness of any leader.

Chapter Four

STRENGTHENING SYSTEMS

CHURCH SYSTEMS

Since the church is referred to as the body of Christ, and since each local church can be viewed as an expression of the whole body, it makes sense that each church has bodily systems just as the human body does. A church is more than just a whole; it is the sum of its parts. How a church is doing can best be answered by asking how various parts of the church are doing. That is the *skillfulness* of David we spoke about in chapter 1. For instance, our church recently went through an extremely trying time when an assorted group of people who had left our congregation over the previous five eyars rallied around their collective displeasure. They were mobilized initially by a disgruntled man who made phone calls claiming to represent our denomination in an investigation of abusive practices at The Coastlands. Because they were unhappy, they decided that the leadership was abusive—an incredibly loaded accusation. Though their hurtful comments and unkind actions against me were deeply distressing to my family and to our pastoral team, their antics had virtually no effect on the rest of the congregation.

In fact, the assault against us served to bond our congregation together even more tightly, and it boosted the levels of morale and affection to their highest point in the eleven-year history of our congregation. It was difficult to answer my pastor friends when they asked me how the church was going. On one hand, I would have to say, "Terrible—the worst ever." But on the other hand, I could truly reply that "(some) things were going great." An attack on one part of the church body does not necessarily affect the other parts, just as an ear infection doesn't inflame the joints.

Bodily growth in humans is retarded and hindered without functioning, developing systems. If the lungs are underdeveloped or if the thyroid malfunctions, the body will not be able to reach its full potential. It is one thing for a child to be born, yet quite another thing for that child to be healthy—meaning that all the child's systems are functioning normally. We will love the child no matter what the child's condition, but we will do whatever we can to improve his or her health.

In the same way, a church must have carefully developed and arranged systems to ensure a healthy congregation. After conception, a person's genetic code automatically governs development of the nine body systems. Not so in the church. Bodily process systems for church do not naturally develop; they must be purposefully tended to and engineered by the church leaders, although not mechanically nor void of divine inspiration. Without properly developed systems, a church will not be able to function and grow on its own.

Let's take a look at the natural body systems and compare them with the sorts of systems a church needs to be effective in problem solving and planning. Just as the human body has nine systems—circulatory, skeletal, muscular, digestive, respiratory, nervous, endocrine, excretory, and reproductive—so a church body has many systems. It isn't enough to keep one or two processes healthy. Paying attention to all the necessary systems of the church is crucial to health, strength, and productivity. If a church is stunted, retarded systems may be at fault.

CIRCULATORY SYSTEM

The purpose of the circulatory system is to convey the nutrients in the blood to every cell in the body and maintain homeostasis (chemical balance and internal equilibrium). When the blood supply is cut off from any part of the body, that part suffers and can eventually die. The same is true in church. For me, paying attention to the circulatory system in church means ensuring that every individual receives care and nurture. I want people to be touched and pastored, shown affection and attention whether they know the more established members of the church or not.

Therefore, I regularly ask myself what we can do to develop more veins, arteries, and capillaries to get adequate blood to every person. *Core group* is a four-letter word in our church. I understand why pastors use the terms *core group* and *fringe group,* but it's possible that people are in the fringe group because a church lacks an adequate circulatory system to get care to them, not necessarily because—as pastors presume—those "fringe" people lack commitment or interest.

While the core group of a church—the ones closest to and most supportive of the church leader—may be receiving adequate attention and nurture, those people outside the inner circle may not be. Typically in a church or group of a hundred adults, the number of people who are receiving enough one-on-one ministry may be only about twenty to thirty-five. Since those are the opinion shapers, the leader mistakenly imagines that everyone is as pleased with the group and is experiencing as much true fellowship as those core people are, when in reality the majority are left out of the loop.

Newcomers often get caught in this disadvantageous predicament. Because they lack the long-term relationships in the church, they aren't getting the same information or ministry attention afforded to people already well established in the congregation. Pastors develop the church circulatory system by supplementing the usual channels of communication and attentiveness with special meetings and activities for visitors.

If I am aware that groups of people in our church are not getting adequate care, I think about ways we can build systems to reach them. We began cell groups so that every person would have somebody with whom he or she could easily get in contact. Cell groups enable us to keep the span of care small enough so that caregivers can attend to the few people in their group and still have time to care for newcomers.

Like any developmental process, our systems need regular refocusing. Recently, as I thought about the circulatory system in our church, I felt that our existing cell groups had lost their incentive to recruit. We had an influx of new people attending the weekend services, but they were not being picked up in the cells. At the time, we had two groups of cell leaders, so I decided to jump-start a third group. Then we shuffled the pastors around, put another pastor in charge of the new group, and started ten new cell groups right away, violating the principle we try to follow of only raising up apprentice leaders. By starting those ten new groups, we gave the new leaders the incentive to grow, and they took in this batch of newer people in the space of about three months.

Keeping the church's circulatory system from clogging requires constant effort. We train people to talk to a variety of people during fellowship times rather than always chatting with the same close friends. I discourage people who know my telephone number from talking to me at church on Sunday, because they can always reach me at another time. I set an example by going to new people to make sure they get welcomed.

Looking at the various systems of the body can help us take a more proactive stance of development in our churches. For instance, by realizing that we would need an ever-increasing number of leaders to adequately supply the increasing number of people coming to The Coastlands, we were forced to confront the issue of leadership development before it became a problem. Cell groups, for example, not only spread care and nurture more evenly throughout the church, they also force the issue of leadership development. More church members are cared for by an increasing number of other church members. If we allowed the cell groups to continue increasing in size rather than in number, we would not really be solving the future need for more leaders. The laypeople who attracted forty to fifty others into their group would not be doing anything to increase the pool of new leaders. Consequently, we restricted the size of any one group to twelve to fourteen adults.

While few people have the gifting to successfully run a cell group of forty to fifty adults, most people can handle a group of twelve. Five groups of ten will provide better circulation than one group of fifty. To reach every member in the church, I needed more capillaries, not more veins. Large public services do distribute consistent teaching throughout the congregation, but they cannot effectively handle all the circulatory needs of the church body. The blood flowing into the left leg is supposed to contain the same elements as the blood reaching the right thumb.

I realized not long ago that in our zeal to get everyone into a cell group, we were getting dangerously close to excluding those who were not ready for that step from receiving an equal supply of nutrients. Maybe they were shy. Perhaps they had been burned by the heavy "shepherding" movement—a misguided application of the biblical principles of authority and submission. Its excesses led to very controlling leaders who *required* submission and obedience from the followers. People felt they needed to get permission for all their choices and decisions. The shepherding movement lost the attitude of servanthood of the leaders.

In any case, some people were not yet willing to enter into a cell group. This was a problem when those people sought out counseling—something we handled almost exclusively through our cell groups.

Staying focused on the circulatory process, I asked myself how we could get the cell groups and the counseling to the shy people since we couldn't get those people to the groups. An answer to the right question is usually the solution to the problem. Process and system thinking offered the right question: How could we get the counseling provided by the cell-group leaders *to* the shy people? The solution was fairly easy: When people not in a cell group requested counseling, we had a cell-group leader call the people, rather than requiring that the people go to the cell group. Imagery here is very helpful. When people come to our church, are we most eager to see them get into the church or to see the church get into them? Are they that food our church absorbs and uses, or are they parts we have a responsibility to supply with nourishment?

SKELETAL SYSTEM

The skeletal system gives structure, shape, and support to the body. Attending to the skeletal system in church means focusing on how we can promote or sustain growth through organization, administration, and structure. This is one of those systems about which there is a great deal of unnecessary debate. Some believers imagine that if a meeting has a planned order, then there is "no room for the Holy Spirit to move." They equate structure with a lack of faith, quoting the verses about not worrying about tomorrow (Matt. 6:34) or about speaking in front of rulers and authorities (Luke 12:11–12). They want to "flow in the Spirit."

A friend of mine who pastors in the Midwest recently told me about a group who left his church because he "wouldn't let God be God." What they meant by such a charge was that they didn't want a planned order of worship and a prepared message each Sunday. They wanted ecstatic manifestations. Other saints commit their *plans* to the Lord in the mistaken hope that he will establish their *ways*. They approach spiritual enterprises as if they are business affairs, wanting to "do things decently and in order."

A body needs bones to keep it from flowing too much—to give it definition and the ability to stand up. Churches need administration, organization, and structure, especially as they grow. Without these elements, many people will get frustrated unnecessarily. An incredibly gifted musician quit our worship team many years ago because he understandably grew tired of unstructured practices that began forty-five minutes late every week.

Many of the nagging problems in church are skeletal problems. For example, in our intern/resident program, which is a cross between short-term missions and Bible college in the context of the local church, we usually have between eight and twelve people at one time. At first we had a staff pastor over the program, but like chronic arthritis, problems nagged the program because the practical aspects were given too little attention. In Acts 6 the apostles faced a similar need for management and appointed others to handle the distribution of food so that they could attend to the ministry of the Word of God and prayer. In our case, instead of appointing a pastor over the intern program, I appointed a single woman as director, and it now works like a well-oiled machine.

As this example reflects, a key development in the skeletal system of our church has been the appointment of staff who are directors rather than pastors. Directors, who are laypeople and mostly women, manage the operation and keep things working. The directors oversee children's ministries, church communications, our intern/residence program, and office management. In our administrative meetings, the directors have equal authority with the pastors except in spiritual matters.

Two other principles promote health in our skeletal system. First, we always staff our weakness. Second, we select staff who are gifted primarily as recruiters and administrators rather than as vocational ministers. Churches are filled with laypeople who have a heart for personal ministry. All they need to "go for it" is delegated permission and an opportunity to be equipped and mobilized. We need more effective directors on staff, not more people who can minister to individual needs.

Without good planning, many otherwise great events can lose their effectiveness. For instance, we had a huge turnout for a barbecue on the last night of vacation Bible school a few years ago, but because we underestimated the amount of chicken we needed and the amount of time it would take to cook it, we drew grumbles from the unsaved parents we most wanted to attract to future events. A little better planning could have better supported what we hoped to accomplish.

Harvest festivals, worship sets, outreaches, youth retreats, facilities maintenance, choir groups, financial management, and a host of other church activities and departments must be given prayerful and thoughtful structure. Good questions for every leader to ask are "What areas of the church seem frustrated or sloppy?" and "Can anything be done to improve the lines of communication or to more clearly organize the effort of everyone involved?"

MUSCULAR SYSTEM

The body's muscular system provides strength, movement, and mobility. When churches are referred to as "strong," I wonder what is meant. Are we talking about their size, their wealth, their visibility, or something else? Unfortunately, big bodies are not always strong, and a wealthy congregation may not necessarily be living up to its potential ("From everyone who has been given much, much will be demanded; and from the one who has been entrusted with much, much more will be asked" [Luke 12:48]). While each pastor ought to decide for his or her own congregation what attributes or measurements best constitute "strength," I believe a church's strength lies in servanthood, which can be measured by the percentage of the congregation that has been effectively mobilized into volunteer activities.

Churches are strong by virtue of their proven capacity to enlist people in the whole mission of the church, not just in listening and giving on Sunday. The more volunteers, the stronger the church. Increasing in strength for the human body requires regular and sustained workouts—"no pain, no gain." A good coach works the players in practice to ready them for the game. An effective pastor is like a coach. Even when athletes get in shape, they don't stay that way without effort. The same is true for church members.

Getting a church in shape takes continuous work and creativity. For instance, our twelve-acre church campus requires a great deal of work and maintenance, and in order to mobilize enough people to do all the work, we need a new plan about every fourteen to eighteen months. We tried "Single Summer Service," in which everyone was asked to give one morning out of the entire summer to work. Then we went to quarterly work parties with huge numbers of people coming at the same time. We stress that we are a "two-service" church: we receive ministry during one service and give it during the other.

One key to high involvement is getting people plugged in where they are best suited. Several years ago I recognized that for the sake of institutional integrity, we needed someone to regularly inventory our office supplies. I didn't want any of our full- or part-time staff to be distracted by this, so I made an announcement one Sunday: "I have an opportunity for someone to serve the church. Before I tell you what the need is, let me describe the kind of person I'm looking for. You'll know you're qualified for this job if one of three things is true: (1) You have cleaned out your desk drawers more than twice in the last twelve months. (2) In the last three months you went to put something away in a closet, but before you could put it away, you decided to totally rearrange the closet. (3) When you are in someone else's home or work space, you think things like *If only he would put this over there, things would work so much better."* Immediately after church three people came up and said, "That's me!" Our need for someone to inventory our materials and supplies matched their disposition and gift mix. For several years those people rotated each week, organizing and doing inventory in our office.

When we think of the muscular system, we tend to think about staffing existing positions and needs: ushers, Sunday school workers, parking attendants. Even if those positions are all filled, however, a huge proportion of the congregation still has nothing to do. When I first moved to Aptos to plant The Coastlands, God told me that I should have the outlook that there wasn't enough to do for everyone who needed to serve. The question isn't just "Are people volunteering?" The question that I discipline myself to keep asking is, "Am I creating enough volunteer positions?" My job is to dream up work and options for volunteers.

We have an incredible number of positions and opportunities at The Coastlands, yet we seem to have no lack of people to fill them, because everybody can find something that satisfies his or her need to serve. I spend a lot of time thinking and praying about individuals in our church, asking, "What is the best role for John? What is his uniqueness and calling? What excites him?"

One woman in our church who recently volunteered to tidy up our office, is a good example of what I mean. When she was working one day, I kidded her, "You get so excited about doing this, you're almost quivering!"

"I know, Pastor, I know," she said. "I love doing this kind of thing!"

The key to a strong muscular system is finding ministry opportunities that excite people. Weakness comes when the wrong people are doing certain jobs or the same few people are doing everything. Strength comes from developing an effective way of identifying gifts, talents, and passions in people and matching them with jobs in the church.

Another practice that has developed our muscular system is building the mentality in the people that they should (1) always be looking for an apprentice to whom they can pass on what they know and (2) always be thinking about doing something else in the future. We tell our pastors, "Your job is to recruit other people.

I'm not impressed by what you do; I'm impressed by what you can get others to do."

The director of our vacation Bible school, to whom we pay $450 a month all year long, exemplifies that attitude. Our annual VBS has expanded into a massive effort, with fifty team leaders and one hundred to two hundred adults volunteering their time for different days of the week. Some of them work on VBS literally all year long. The director spends all year mobilizing two dozen underdirectors who, in turn, do the bulk of the volunteer recruiting in their particular area of assignment—nursery care, activities, snack bar, equipment, and so on.

I believe God is trying to alert pastors to the importance of servanthood as an articulated and vital component of healthy churches. The reason congregational volunteering is such a constant need—more Sunday school workers, more office helpers, more food bank workers—is because leaders are supposed to devote more thoughtful prayer and energy to cultivating a servant's heart in their congregants.

DIGESTIVE SYSTEM

The body's digestive system is concerned with receiving, digesting, and absorbing food, and the spiritual counterpart to the digestive system is the teaching ministry at church. When we look at the church digestive system we focus on questions such as, "What is the Lord trying to teach us?" and "What does he want to teach us about where we are going to be in the year ahead?"

Since most pastors are trained to feed their flock the Word of God, this system is usually the best developed of all the systems in churches. In fact, feeding the people is the solution most often considered by church leaders. Like new parents, pastors tend to overfeed. And like eager hosts, pastors tend to equate how many helpings of food the guests eat with how good a time those guests are having. Pastors urge people to eat more and more, presuming that "a good, square meal" will take care of whatever ails them.

Because pastors already put so much effort into maintaining this necessary system, little can be done to improve it at most churches—except perhaps to do more to enable the people to get better at supplementing their diet by feeding themselves. I try to give regular pointers and explanations about how I arrived at a conclusion from the Bible text I'm teaching from. This can be little asides like, "Ministry will often be painful" (from the word *agonizomai* in Colossians 1:29), or somewhat lengthy statements that provide handles by which average readers can hold on to passages.

For instance, it became clear to me that most of the people in our church were not very familiar with the Old Testament. Since I knew that they would neither be interested in nor remember (for their future readings) the usual sort of "Bible survey" material I was tempted to give them, I selected an unusual passage from an Old Testament book each week for over a year to convince the congregation that there were all sorts of stories they never learned in Sunday school. Beyond that I gave a five- to seven-minute introduction to each book, designed to maximize their future readings. I encouraged them to write a few words in their Bibles on the first page of the book of the week. Here are a couple of examples:

> *Numbers* is the book of arrangements; it tells us that God has an order for life and a proper positioning for us just as he situated the different tribes in their encampment. That is why the murmurings of Aaron and Miriam, as well as the rebellion of Korah and the sons of Eliab, are so central to the narrative. The people of God face constant temptation to lead themselves and to make their own arrangements for life.

> *Ecclesiastes* is not the depressive musing of a hopeless person but a reminder that we should worship the Lord who lives beyond the sun—the sun under which all is vanity and "striving after the wind." Every person will eventually grow disillusioned with life unless he or she is linked to life beyond the sun.

Our assignment as leaders is to make the Word of God less mysterious and more accessible to our congregations. These simple introductions give people a reference point. God teaches us today what we need to know for tomorrow. If we only look at our current situation and ask what we need to learn, we miss much of what God wants to teach us. By giving our people handles for their future reading, we emphasize that point.

The digestive system is a good example of the overlap that often exists between the spiritual and the natural. Although this book emphasizes the practical side of leadership, it will not do so exclusively. Systems and processes are spiritual! When I look at the digestive system, I not only think about what I myself will be teaching, but about how the church can be best organized to feed our people a healthy diet. We only have one service a week at which I teach, and recently I felt we needed more ways to get teaching into the body. It occurred to me that people usually learn the most when they study to teach rather than when they are taught. If my true passion is to get people to learn more, instead of my doing more teaching, I ought to enlist more teachers.

So we started an adult seminar offered every other Tuesday night, and we invited, as our teachers, men and women whom we felt had a handle on Scripture and perhaps had gone through something that made their teaching their life message. The adult seminars turned out to be extremely successful, with groups ranging in size from 12 to 120 people.

RESPIRATORY SYSTEM

The respiratory system processes oxygen to the body. In the church, the respiratory system is the breath and inspiration of the Holy Spirit. I often ask myself, "What is the Holy Spirit doing in us right now? How does he want to breathe inspiration into us? How does he want to give life-giving oxygen?"

Every church needs a fresh breath of the Spirit. Without that newness, things will grow stale. What can a leader do to allow for and to encourage the Holy Spirit's Word and work in a congregation? We might solicit letters from our elders, asking them to give us their sense of what the Lord is saying to the church. Or, in reading respected Christian journals, we might find a theme that strikes a responsive chord in our heart. Prophetic words, pictures received while praying, along with scriptural passages and phrases, will also alert us to what the Holy Spirit is doing in our midst.

Just as God gave direction to the churches in the book of Revelation, he has a direction for us. I want to have ears to hear, to know what the Spirit of Jesus is saying to our church. We can have theologically sound churches, but they are dry bones unless we are in step with the Spirit's leading.

Several years ago God's leading surprised me. Although The Coastlands is known as a church that mobilizes people for service—roughly 85 percent of regular attendees are involved in some sort of ministry or small group—I felt God was telling us to rest. We had just renovated the old convent we lease. I knew God wasn't calling us to just the usual "everybody's tired" kind of rest. I felt prompted by the Lord to teach people how to enter into God's rest, so I did a four-part series on Sabbath and gave people permission to slow down. I had to work hard to remove the feelings of guilt that some people have if they are not working hard in church. We said no to additional services, and when in doubt, we threw out programs. We virtually did nothing but the barest of essentials for seven months. That time brought oxygen and inspiration to the congregation. When that season was over, we cranked it back up again and had mass mobilization. These kinds of prophetic breaths facilitate a congregation's ability to give themselves to what the Lord is doing in their midst.

NERVOUS SYSTEM

The nervous system is our discernment, our ability to sense what is happening in our body. In the church it is different from, though often related to, the respiratory system—what the Holy Spirit is inspiring, saying, or doing. Sometimes we will sense not a work of the Spirit, but a work of evil, like pain and sickness, multiple cases of adultery, a wave of gossip and misunderstanding, and so on. This opposition or "attack" against the church must be responded to with prayer and biblical instruction.

What alerts the church to danger or to the surrounding prevailing conditions? How does your church become aware of needs within the body or in the culture around it? What prophetic sense or discernment gives you confidence that the church is healthy or on the right track? These questions frame the spiritual counterparts of the nervous system.

What happens in the natural realm often points back to something spiritual. A few months ago I felt a personal sense of discouragement and exhaustion. Since I'm not prone to depression, this was very unusual. Every Christian leader goes through deserts, and so at first I thought, *Never mind. Just keep going. Hallelujah!* But as days passed, I sensed that this was something more than periodic dryness, so I did a personal inventory: *Okay, what's going on in my life?* After a thorough examination, I didn't find anything particularly sinful to explain what I was feeling. So I shared my feelings with my wife and a few other people, and I heard story after story from them of other people in the church who felt beat-up spiritually but couldn't identify the cause.

One woman in our church is extremely discerning (I call her my long-range radar). During this time, she told me offhandedly of a strange dream in which she sensed a presence trying to harm her. She said, "I thought I even heard its name—something like Raffa or Raffta."

I don't give that kind of thing too much credence one way or the other without further confirmation, so my only response—aside from an outward expression of gratitude for her concern and thoughts was, *That's interesting.*

Two nights later I was reading in Isaiah 35, and I came across verse 3: "Encourage the exhausted, and strengthen the feeble" (NASB). That seemed like no big deal even though I knew I was exhausted and a bit on the feeble side. What caught my eye was not the verse itself but a handwritten word next to the verse. For years I have been in the habit of writing notes from my personal studies in the margin of my Bible, and there in the margin I had previously written the Hebrew word for "exhausted," *rapheh*, which also can be translated "slack" or "consumed."

Whoa! I decided that this Scripture must be something we needed to look into as a church. We had a problem that God was helping me to understand. That discovery led to six weeks of sermons about God's promise to visit our desert place and make it blossom, based on Isaiah 35. We found that incredible lessons can be learned in the midst of the desert. Each week I had record numbers of people coming up and saying, "This is right where I am; you've been reading my mail." We sold more tapes of this series than of any previous series.

I see this example less as something the devil was doing and more as God pointing us to our desert, blighted places and giving us his promise of what he would do to restore us. Nervous system discernment isn't always focused on problems, though that is a big part of it. It is easy to see what the devil is up to, hard to see what God is up to. It's more important to find out what God wants to do in the thick of our problems.

My efforts at discernment are not always mystical or spiritual. A very helpful exercise is to list the major issues that are confronting the church—not just the obvious ones of finances, staff, facilities, and so on. What do you see when you look around? What do you hear? And then consider the key leaders in your church. What issues do they face? Where are they supposed to walk, and what is preventing them from being able to do so? One style of business management is referred to as "management by walking around." As the name implies, the leader spends lots of time wandering around observing, asking questions and answering them, and talking with rank-and-file workers. This is a digestive system process.

ENDOCRINE SYSTEM

The hormones of the endocrine system are the chemical control system of the body. Hormones stimulate cells to bring growth, health, and balance. The endocrine system regulates various organs. The amount of physical substance actually involved is very small, yet without the additives carried throughout the body, the body wouldn't work properly. On the spiritual side of church, the endocrine system is made up of intangible activities like prayer, faith, and the prevailing atmosphere of love and servanthood. On the organic side, it is things like the core values of the church and its ministry philosophy, including such values as servanthood, accountability, innovation, openness, forgiveness, supportiveness, and empowerment.

No matter how mature a Christian may be in a general sense, it does not mean that he or she values the same things that your church values. If, however, all the leaders do not share the same values, the body will be thrown out of balance internally. Although there is not one right set of ministry perspectives for all churches, the ministry ought to be consistent. If your church wants to reach the unchurched, it can't do so by clinging to a music perspective that values the old hymns of the church above contemporary songs. And you can't claim to be passionate for missions without somehow managing to work it into your budget.

At our church we put more emphasis on developing people for new ministry capacities than we do on getting the job done right. That means we have to live with mistakes. If we don't want mistakes to happen, we have to minimize our interest in thrusting people into ministry responsibilities for which they are not as trained as they will one day be. We do, of course, watch people's faithfulness in little things, as well as their character, before we entrust them with considerable ministry responsibility. But since our goal is to mobilize an increasing number of people into significant ministry, we will necessarily sacrifice competent monopolies on various ministry roles. In other words, we want more than one person to be capable of filling a role.

The question suggested by the endocrine system in the church process is "Where are we running thin in living out our key values?" As more newcomers began to attend our church, I noticed that people were scattering farther apart rather than sitting together. I made comments now and then to encourage more togetherness but realized I was losing that battle. Then I decided that we needed to reintroduce the hormone of togetherness. I began to weave that theme into my teaching, and I talked to the ushers about roping off the back of the sanctuary until the front filled up.

I have found that one of the key ways to introduce such hormone shots into the church is by use of word pictures. For instance, one core value for us is believing in people and the future God has for them. I often describe people as mountains composed of a lot of dirt, but within that dirt there are precious gems. It is our job to find the precious material in people: "Just because you have seen someone's dirt, doesn't mean you know all that they have in them."

EXCRETORY SYSTEM

Just as the human body must have an open system to eliminate waste, so the church must effectively eliminate unhealthy
things. People need help to be healed emotionally, to have the
traumas of their lives and the damage of other people's sins and
their own misdeeds released. They need to experience forgiveness
and the letting go of the past, of sinful habits, of bondage, and of
distorted viewpoints. They also need to release anger and bitter-
ness. Abused people need to get beyond the victim mentality or the
desire for revenge.

For these reasons, The Coastlands has placed a high priority
on our counseling ministry. We have found that a church doesn't
have to employ expensive, professional counselors conducting therapy on the basis of psychological models, to effectively help people.
We train appropriately gifted laypeople to counsel in teams of
three—an experienced counselor and two apprentices. We rely on
prayer, Scripture, and the Holy Spirit, and we are so desperate to
find answers for people, that God has truly been setting them free.
We have experienced "the more excellent way" of love for people.
Rather than keeping the counseling "professional," we have pur-
sued solutions through profound love for those being counseled.

Our current counseling system developed in the late 1980s,
when a wave of moral failures by prominent church leaders hit the
press. I felt we needed to protect ourselves by setting a policy that
male pastors would no longer conduct ongoing counsel with
women. First, though, we had to set up a system that would
ensure that all our women would be cared for. Therefore, I asked
two women in our church who had counseled others extensively
with my wife and me, "If I could confine all of your counseling to
one five-hour period a week, would you be interested?"

"You bet," they both replied. Everyone knew how good they
were at counseling, and thus they were receiving calls at all hours
of the day. A set schedule would be a welcome relief.

"All right, then," I said; "each of you come to the church one
day a week for five hours, and I will give you a team of other
women to work with you and be trained by you."

One team came on Tuesday, the other on Thursday. After some time, I took the apprentice counselors from each group, made each a leader, and gave them two more apprentices with an aptitude for counseling; so we then had four counseling teams. After three years we had twelve teams of counselors helping people during the day and evening. Now the bulk of counseling is done by teams of laypeople working closely with the leaders of the small group the counselee is in, under the supervision of our pastors.

The excretory system has corollaries in church other than just a counseling ministry. One of the most common mistakes made by pastors is trying to hold on to everyone in the church and fighting the very normal process of letting go of people who want to move on to another church. We cannot pastor everyone, and it is a myth to imagine that everyone who has ever been a part of our church should always be a part of it. The role of any church in the lives of its members is only temporary and partial. Church is supposed to help fill people's lives with more and more of the Lord—not vice versa. If leaders are not careful, they will confuse loyalty to them with obedience to God.

We must be willing to let go of people when it is time. Actually, congregations grow more as a consequence of who leaves than of who stays. It is quite normal for people to disembark from a train before others get on. If they are prevented from leaving, it will likely also prevent others from climbing aboard. I have discovered that the best leaders for the church at one stage in its life may not necessarily be the right ones for another stage. The more fluid and flexible our church leadership roles can remain, the better.

What programs have outlived their effectiveness? Who has remained in the same position, doing the same things for many years? Are there situations or problems that have persisted in the church that require a concerted measure of fasting and prayer? These are questions of a healthy excretory system.

REPRODUCTIVE SYSTEM

The human body is designed to reproduce. Though some babies are called "accidents," all we really mean is that we did not expect an activity that we know can produce a child to do so *in a particular case.* Without the activity, accidents wouldn't happen. Some people teach that all healthy organisms reproduce and say that if a church is healthy, reproduction will occur naturally. But that is like telling a married couple to spend all their time working out at the health club and watching their diet. Having babies is a bit more involved than that.

Churches need to purposefully engage in activities that lead to reproduction. Are your cell groups designed to multiply or to remain intact? Do you have plans to look for potential church planters and groom them, or is the goal to hang on to all the gifted leaders because there are so few of them? Is there room in the leadership circle for any more emerging leaders? What about new ministry ventures—how do people receive permission to "go for it"?

Process thinking, when focused on the reproductive system, will give pastors another great reason to let go of key leaders. If they were really doing a good job, it will probably take two or three people to replace them. That is reproduction! Instead of viewing it as a crisis, pastors can see it as an opportunity to multiply. A few months ago while I was visiting one of our daughter churches in Fort Collins, I was again struck with the need to send our best into the world. At the first pastors' meeting after I returned to Aptos, I told my pastors to really ask God about pioneering! One month later, my key associate pastor, Gary, who has been with me since we started The Coastlands, told me that God had called him to pioneer in Nashville. Whew! That is an incredible development—one that will require an entire reconfiguration of our staff and ministry structures to accommodate.

We will need four people to fill the gap he is leaving. But isn't that a testimony to his success? And isn't it an opportunity to release new people into the ministry roles that he was keeping unavailable to others because of his gifts and diligence? When Gary and his wife, Bonny, leave in two months, the kingdom will have gained a new senior pastor in Nashville, a new administrator, a new financial director, and two new lay ministers in Aptos. That's what I call success!

Not all growth is numeric; but if a small church is going to tout its commitment to "quality not quantity," it had better show that its people will have more chance to learn new ministry skills than they would in a large church. The size of a body is not the determining factor in its ability to reproduce.

Individuals, cell groups, and churches maintain the best health when they reproduce. In my experience the key to strengthening the reproductive system of the church has been having a long-range vision and plan, looking ahead to what can be done over the next five or more years. In our vacation Bible school, for example, one adult leader is responsible for eight children, and each adult also has a counselor in training, a junior high or early high school student who enjoys working with grade school kids. Our counselor-in-training program has been in existence for five years now, and some of the young people have grown up and are leading teams on their own. Because of the counselor-in-training program, we will never have trouble getting team leaders in the future. I encourage all the workers in our church to find apprentices, train them, then go to another ministry.

One problem we are having right now in our church is the result of a failure to look ahead. We once had an abundance of counseling teams and even had to let some go because we had too many, but lately we have been in need of more teams—especially for men. It is a nice problem to have so many men wanting to receive counsel, but it is still a problem. The difficulty arose because we weren't identifying and training enough entry-level counselors to serve with experienced counselors and later become lead counselors.

I have also found that planting new churches requires a long-range perspective. At The Coastlands I always have my eye out for potential church planters. Once I identify such a person or couple, I woo them for over a year, talking about the importance of planting churches and dropping hints. It takes two to three years for an *identified* pioneer pastor prospect to get ready to start a church, so unless I have a long-range perspective, I will miss opportunities to recruit future pastors.

A LITTLE HERE AND THERE

The comparison of body systems to church systems shows how important systems are to the health of an organization. There are many other systems in a church, from minor administrative systems such as handling the daily mail to major pastoral systems such as following up on new converts. The point is, we need to think systems, build systems, and put people in charge of systems. And we also need to monitor their health. If there is a problem, we must ask the Lord what systems are needed to correct it. Systems thinking is process thinking. Systems are tributaries feeding into the whole church process.

A woman who recently dedicated her life to Christ told me one day how she perceived our church. "The first thing I noticed about this place," she said, "was that you mean what you say about serving. I can't believe the way everybody around here serves."

Her comment gratified me, because it said that our church body is generally healthy. Sure, we have our aches and pains and occasional sickness just like everybody else, but overall, the systems are functioning, the body parts are working together, and we are reflecting "the fullness of him who fills everything in every way."

Thinking about all the different things a leader might do to develop or enhance the body systems of the church process can be overwhelming. May I suggest that you concentrate on one system each week and come up with one proactive change for the church from your thinking about that system. Over time—remember that church is a process—you will be amazed at what a big difference can be accomplished by a continuous string of little differences. And you will probably discover that you have many more parts in place than you realize. By focusing on how those already working parts can be better integrated into systems and processes, you will be able to see real progress in your church.

Chapter Five

COAXING CHANGE

eadership is not a maintenance role, for one cannot legitimately lead people to where they already are. The status quo cannot be an organization's goal or purpose, and it must be interpreted and evaluated by leadership in terms of the real goal the organization is trying to achieve. Truly effective leaders are change agents, constantly repositioning people, programs, resources, objectives, and whole organizations to best accomplish their institutional mission. Accomplishing legitimate, meaningful change may well be the real test of leadership.

LESSONS FROM SPRING CLEANING

In the process of spring cleaning, my wife felt compelled to switch the contents of two drawers in our bathroom. These drawers are of identical shape and configuration, and they sit side by side to the right of the sink. Prior to the "great cleaning," the toothbrushes and the toothpaste were kept in the left-hand drawer, and the hairbrushes had their place in the front of the right-hand drawer. I could walk into the bathroom and find my toothbrush without thinking. Ever since my wife changed those drawers, though, I have had to concentrate to find what I need. Rather than routinely reaching for my toothbrush, I must now strategize my actions. Since it seems that no matter which drawer I choose first is always the wrong one, I open one drawer without looking in it, close it, and open the second drawer. Without fail, the second drawer contains what I need.

Change is uncomfortable. It forces us to think. It complicates normal routines by breaking our unconscious rhythms and habits. It forces us to learn new skills, and it causes disagreements and insecurity. Change is disconcerting, personally and corporately. Because of the potential conflict it can cause, church leaders often avoid introducing change in their congregations. They think, *Why not keep the program and keep the peace?*

STATUS QUO IS NOT AN OPTION

Church leaders have discovered—either through painful experiences or careful deduction—that their people do not like change. People are suspicious of and resistant to change. For some reason, they generally conclude that they will come out the worse for it; therefore, they believe a familiar state of affairs, even a bad one, is always to be preferred to an unknown one. This is where leadership must step up in the church. Our assignment is to carefully lead people in the ways and truth of the Lord. While we want to be on good terms with people, as far as it is possible, "We are not trying to please men but God, who tests our hearts" (1 Thess. 2:4).

The possibility of trouble is a feeble excuse for avoiding needed change. Do people in church jump for joy when they first learn about tithing? No, we have to explain why it is important to their well-being. How about other crucial subjects—turning the other cheek, repenting, confessing, and dying to self? There are few aspects of the kingdom of God that people like in the natural. God's ways can be disconcerting to our natural man. No wonder, then, that repentance—change—plays such a critical role in spiritual development. God says, "My thoughts are not your thoughts, neither are your ways my ways" (Isa. 55:8). So, guess whose ways will have to change? The spiritual potency of change may very well explain people's resistance to it.

Staying the same is not an option in the church, for two reasons. First, *change fulfills God's purpose for the believer.* We can summarize much of the New Testament in one sentence: "You are going to change," says the Lord. Another translation may be, "You are going to die." That is the small print at the bottom of the contract when we give our hearts to Jesus, and it explains many of the unexplainable things in our Christian experience. In hard times we want to say, "God, what are you trying to do—kill me?" Up in heaven God nods. Of course that's the program. He allows us to die, so that it is no longer we who live, but Christ; and the life we live in the flesh is lived supernaturally by faith (Gal. 2:20). Death and change bring life. Christians who try to avoid change can end up frustrating God's purposes.

According to Romans 8:28–29, God works in all circumstances for the good of his children, but people rarely focus on what that "good" is. It is not comfort and ease—everything working out as we had hoped. The highest good is for us to be shaped in the likeness of Jesus Christ. The good is transformational, a metamorphosis. God is like the great McGyver in the sky; he uses every available circumstance, relationship, and resource in our lives to change us. Certainly that includes using the church.

Unfortunately, human nature is such that if our circumstances do not change, we tend to stay the same. How can church leaders imagine, then, that doing the same thing week after week in church will foster discipleship? Einstein's definition of insanity goes something like this: "An insane person is someone who keeps doing the same thing over and over, waiting for a different result." How odd, then, that most arguments against change are based on claims that the change is not reasonable or easy.

Almost any change is better for people than none at all. Change forces us to depend more on God than on habit, to think about why we do what we do. When a particular change is especially resisted in church on no biblical or spiritual grounds, that may be a good clue that God wants it. Reasons why people do not want the change are far more telling than the simple fact that they do not want it.

I am not suggesting that we make changes simply to make changes. Making ill-advised changes is no more sane than repeating the same ineffective procedures. My point is that change should not be avoided just because it is a change and people in the church may not like it *at first*. It goes back to church as a process—an ongoing development (spell that c-h-a-n-g-e) of the entire church environment to promote the growth and maturity (radical change) in people. In a broken world where everything keeps wearing down and dying, new and different works must be initiated.

The second reason that staying the same is not an option for the church is that *our society is in continual flux*. Analysts in the business community believe the world has passed into a new era of commerce and communication. No agreement has yet been reached about what to name it or about how it works. At this point we can only observe the trends and emerging realities, such as the preeminence of information and convenience as consumer values, increased internationalization, participative management style, ethnic diversification rather than unification, digital conversion and data storage, staggering consumer debts, and so on. More emphasis is being placed on process thinking than on product thinking; we are moving away from the industrial-manufacturing-of-goods mentality toward a mindset of developing and empowering people. In the industrial model, people produce products; in the postindustrial model, processes and products promote a better way of life for people.

People today are growing more and more accustomed to being privileged consumers—picking and choosing what they believe will be most to their advantage or will serve them. To the extent that a local church can present itself as a meaningful service to people who want a better life, it will flourish in these times.

Future shock is here. Volatility is the norm. Everything—assumptions, values, technologies, the economy, entertainment—is changing at the speed of a computer command. If a local church refuses to find an appropriate cultural equivalent for its message in twenty-first-century America (which is a foreign country compared to 1980s America), it will become an isolated enclave of expatriates living out of touch with the world around it.

The postindustrial age (I prefer the term *quotidian,* meaning "daily," because every day things are different from the day before) bears little similarity to the agrarian age or to the industrial age. To relate well to the people of the quotidian age, the church will need to shed the characteristics that developed in response to the realities of the agrarian and industrial ages. Table 5.1 shows the differences in each of these three periods.

Table 5.1

	Preindustrial (Agrarian)	Industrial	Postindustrial (Quotidian)
Outcomes	produce, materials	products, commodities	processes, technologies
Market	local, geographic	mass, product demand	individual, customized
Expansion	physical trade, more resources	population segments, niches	research breakthroughs
Work Schedule	seasonal, repetition of the past	structured, repetition of the present	flexible, anticipation of the future
Workplace Structure	solo, familial	hierarchical, authoritative	collegial, networked, flexible

Let us look at the implications these changes have for how we lead our churches.

Outcomes

The industrial age combined raw materials (the stand-alone focus of the agrarian age) to make what did not exist naturally. People's lives became vastly more complicated with each invention of material objects—engines, radios, machines. Items were designed, mechanized, and produced.

Churches learned to offer products and resources and programs rather than just "a place to grow." Choirs, cassettes, Bible studies, and church services themselves were manufactured by the church to be consumed by the parishioner. They were spiritual commodities in tune with the industrial age.

In the quotidian era, people are focused much more on processes and qualities than on material things or situations. They expect convenience and efficiency. They prize information and service more than physical objects. Thus they will judge a church service more on the basis of how long the service runs overtime or on how easy it is to find a parking spot. How the sermon personally impacts them means more than how beautifully the soloist sings. What services churches provide will soon mean more than what products they offer.

Market

Mass production made way for mass marketing and mass consumption. A product everyone needs or wants can be identically produced and sold to everyone, but with the increase in the number of products and their producers, consumers have come to have more and more choices about which brand or model they like most. We are not content to drive the standard Model-T. We want the make, model, options package, and color that suits our taste.

In the quotidian age, matching preferences with products seems to be almost an inalienable right. Thus, mass customization has replaced mass production. Modular shelves and clothing, model homes that can be built in various combinations of rooms, personal preference profiles for frequent fliers and rental car customers—these are quotidian necessities. The mass market has been replaced with masses of individual markets.

For the most part, churches still offer one main and uniform product to their parishioners. Multiple service times, home cell groups, and a variety of ministry groups that cater to those of a certain age or marital status are good approaches to the quotidian consumer. Church leaders might also think of ways to individualize the instruction process; for instance, a pastor might package different series of ten to fifteen tapes from marriage seminars he or she has taught over the past five years to use in counseling. The set of tapes for single moms would be much different from the set for those in premarriage counseling.

The very call of the church to "make disciples" is a highly individualized assignment. Rather than resisting the social shift from industrial mass production to quotidian individualization, the church should welcome the opportunity to minister to the unique needs of people just as the God who knows and loves everyone in the world remains intently focused on the needs of individuals.

Work Schedule

In the agrarian age, farmers repeated a seasonal cycle of sowing and reaping. Their work was dictated by the time of year, so annual events and dates had great significance. With the coming of the industrial age, factory workers followed a daily schedule, usually performing endlessly repetitive actions—say, attaching front bumpers on cars. Seasons became less meaningful, as did festivals related to harvest. Holidays began to mark historic or political events rather than seasonal changes.

Farmers had to sow all their seed before "the rains came"— not a rigid or well-defined deadline. Within the broad seasonal constraints, farmers could manage their own time. The industrial age brought with it far more structure and definition; deadlines, quotas, and hierarchical structures ensured that workers were doing their jobs on time. It was the age of time clocks and job descriptions.

A quick look at the church calendar will tell you which age your church most resembles. The more seasonal or annual your events and programs are, the more your church fits in the agrarian age mentality. Some annual celebrations—like Christmas and Easter— will always be highlighted because they portray the essence of the truth of Jesus Christ. But other annual activities in our churches may be out of sync with the realities of people's busy schedules.

When church leaders plan meetings or activities three times per year or even once a month, it may look good on a calendar— evenly spread out—but those events may occur during a week already maxed out by more spontaneous or unexpected activities. The quotidian age, with its incredible lack of structure and predictability means we may need to give churchgoers more than one opportunity to attend an event—or more grace for not attending the one opportunity we gave them.

HOLDING STEADY OR STAYING ON COURSE

Suppose you're sailing a small boat on a lake and you want to reach a dock on the opposite side. It's a windy day, and the lake is fed by a large river that causes strong cross-currents. What is the surest way to miss your destination? Never adjust the angle of the sail or rudder.

In a changing environment, continuing to do the same thing guarantees that you will veer far off course. Nevertheless, tying the sail and rudder into a single position is precisely what some of us church leaders want to do. Instead of fixing our sights on the destination across the lake, our eyes attend to the boat and its passengers. We don't want to rock the boat or argue with others about the position of the sail, so we commend the virtues of peace, faithfulness, and holding steady. Having lost sight of the destination, we don't realize how far off course we have gone. All we care about is holding steady. But because things keep changing, we have to keep changing things in order to really change things. Instead of playing catch-up, we need to head off changes at the pass. Like the men of Issachar, we need to understand the times and know what we should do (see 1 Chron. 12:32). As spiritual leaders, we can be prophetic about our society and anticipate the changes necessary in our churches.

For example, in the economy of present-day society, time and space are becoming elements of the highest value. Anything that saves time or space has value. Next-day delivery, faster microprocessors, quick oil-change shops, and fast-food restaurants are valued for the time they save us. Time is money. The complaint "This is taking too long" will be uttered more and more by consumers. The drive to make computers and phones smaller, offices more functional, and appliances less bulky comes from the increasing demand for more space. In the next century, time and space will be two crucial issues for the church. No one will have enough of them.

Church leaders in this new era will have to think much more about time and space when they plan. Long-range planning will have to do more than just rely on evenly balancing the calendar. Soccer practice, car repairs, vet visits, and doctor appointments fill people's "spare" time. Even though the leaders' retreat happens only once a year, it may fall on a weekend that follows the monthly men's breakfast, the quarterly Sunday school training night, and the pre-planning meeting for next spring's youth mission to Mexico.

Last year I had some essential things to cover in a certain leaders' meeting. In times past I would have announced weeks in advance, "Don't go away on the weekend of July 14. Put that date on your calendars for an important leaders' meeting." Instead, I scheduled three separate dates for the identical meeting. "I know you have tight schedules," I announced, "so we're offering this meeting three times. Please make it a priority to attend one of these meetings." Over 94 percent of our leaders attended one of the sessions. I had to spend more of my time to save theirs, but it was worth it to me. That is the kind of change churches must make in the years to come. Schedule, routine, and structure are giving way to change, anticipation, and spontaneity—a good opportunity for us to be "instant, in season and out."

I am amazed at how Christian leaders imagine that their churches are immune to the plagues that hinder other organizations. They seem to forget that though the church is a spiritual entity, it is also housed in a natural structure. To ignore the organizational life of a church—that has natural, organic components to it—is to be short-sighted at best and presumptuous at worst. It is a fatal error for powerful spiritual leaders to forget their own flesh's vulnerability. The fact that we participate in spiritual activity and effect supernatural transformation in the lives of others does not change the fact that our natural bodies are still subject to the laws that govern this broken planet. As Paul told the Corinthians, "We have this treasure in earthen vessels" (2 Cor. 4:7 NASB).

Organizations, like people, are subject to several natural laws that govern their lives. One example is the law of renewal. Every human organization has a predictable life cycle. Organizations have an innovative stage, a growth stage, a plateau, and a decline. Other writers have described this life cycle as "mission, movement, museum, mausoleum." An organization must reinvigorate itself through change, or it will ultimately die. People used to say, "If it's not broken, don't fix it." Now organizational experts say, "If it's not broken, it soon will be obsolete." For example, the frequency that many churches hold services is based on the agrarian model, developed in an age when people didn't have much to do on Sunday. Since transportation was slower, people came to church Sunday morning, stayed for a great picnic and Sunday school in the afternoon, and then stuck around for an evening service before riding home in the wagon.

We no longer live in an agrarian society, and even in rural America people don't have the discretionary time they once did. Churches that hold Sunday night services shouldn't necessarily stop doing so, but they should be clear about the reason for doing so. Additionally, they should take steps to keep from communicating to parishioners that being a dedicated Christian requires attending church a certain number of times per week. Churches that stress attending every service may be forcing people to make decisions they shouldn't have to make and come to conclusions that aren't necessarily true, such as, "I guess I'm not a committed Christian because I really can't come to the midweek service."

On the other hand, when a church meets only once a week, it loses valuable instruction and activity that will need to be supplied some other way. Corporate intercession, a key element in most vital midweek services, might be maintained by monthly days of prayer and fasting, for instance.

In a time-squeezed culture, how can we get more teaching into people without gathering them to a church service several times a week? One idea I'm toying with is producing a monthly "insomnia pack" of audio teaching tapes for those who can't sleep. It would include inductive Bible study and comments from me on tape or on paper. By making one of these available each month, we would have the potential of adding twelve teaching series into the life of our church family without requiring that people come to church. In preparation for next summer, I plan to produce three teaching tapes to be taken on vacation. They will be more personable than a sermon and will offer insight into where I see the church heading in the fall. People should enjoy listening to them on a long drive between vacation spots.

HISTORIC CHANGE

A quick look at history will prove that almost every great leader and organization has somehow been involved with change, either initiating it or capitalizing on it. Organizations that try to maintain the status quo sooner or later lose out. If that has always been true, how much more so in our age of breathtaking change?

Of all people, Christians should be warm to the idea of change. We are taught to pray for *daily* bread, not last week's bread, just as the Israelites ate manna that came one day at a time. God says he will do a new thing. We, of all people, are positioned to embrace what is relevant for today and tomorrow.

Shifting the sails for changing winds doesn't mean compromising or watering down the gospel. Paul says, "I have become all things to all men so that by all possible means I might save some" (1 Cor. 9:22). He shows that we must present the gospel in a way that makes sense to our culture. Our mistake is that we easily confuse the message with the medium; we equate sociocultural patterns and methods with the essence of the gospel. Church has been an ever-changing institution, adapting from the catacombs to the cathedral, from the local parish to the revival center.

Because the church is not primarily a physical entity, it has incredible flexibility and adaptability. The message of Jesus' crucifixion and resurrection can be told through seeker-sensitive dramas each week in converted warehouses or through personal testimonies at a ladies' auxiliary bake sale. Christmas performances of the children's choir are vehicles to touch the dads who rarely come to church; so are church sports teams and Promise Keepers conventions. The more we move away in our thinking from "church" being a place and a specific event that starts and finishes Sunday morning, the more we will be able to utilize the God-intended flexibility of presenting the pure truth to the world.

EASING THE WAY

Embracing the necessity of change doesn't make it any easier to implement. Change is always difficult and often painful. Because there are usually risks—sometimes huge risks—we must pursue change with wisdom. Often people resist a leader's efforts to institute change not because of the change itself but because of the unwise way in which the leader goes about the process: the leader is dictatorial, inconsiderate, impetuous. We need to have regard for the pain that changes may cause and do what we can to ease the discomfort. Below are several guidelines for introducing change in ways that are the least traumatic for our followers.

Show how the change better accomplishes the church's agreed-upon mission and values. Any changes we propose should be in keeping with the mission the leaders have already hammered out together. (If you work out a mission statement early on, you will agree on and claim ownership of what is important before specific controversial issues are at stake.) A leader's job is to help people overcome the natural tendency to forget the church's mission and values.

Going back to the sailboat analogy, a good leader will communicate that he or she is still headed toward the same dock on the other side of the lake. The leader might say, "I know it looks like we're changing everything by adjusting the sail and rudder, but if you look up, you'll discover that we have been blown off course. The changes I propose put us back on course toward our destination."

One obstacle, for instance, to churches starting Saturday night services is the number of new volunteers required to usher, sing, and teach in children's ministries. In many churches that would be a negative. When we began Saturday night services, I communicated that as a positive, since one of our values is mobilizing and empowering people. We saw the need to double the number of people involved in teaching Sunday school as a grand opportunity. When I told the congregation about the change, I talked about how exciting it was to find new things for people to do for the sake of the kingdom. As much as any individual might not want to do the serving him- or herself, they all agreed that serving is good for others. Appealing to that value, I dealt proactively with the potential controversy over the change.

Show how the change meets felt needs. Another job for a true leader is to help people see how a particular change is not only good for the kingdom but also for their own spiritual well-being and growth.

In chapter 4 I shared how The Coastlands counseling ministry to women came about: two women who had already been doing a great deal of one-on-one counseling began to counsel in teams of three—one experienced and two apprentice counselors. They then split off into other teams. When I initially presented this idea to these two popular counselors, they resisted it until I presented the proposed change in terms of their felt needs. I knew that these women's phones rang all week long with calls from women who wanted counsel, so I said, "If I could confine all your counseling to one five-hour period a week, during the day, with no one bugging you at any other time, would you be interested?"

"You bet!" they both replied. Their husbands were especially interested!

God is good and upright. His paths are lovingkindness and truth, and in his presence is fullness of joy. Since he is always intent on our good, it must be true that what he asks us to do will be good for us. A wise leader learns to look for that match between what needs doing and what will bless the people.

Dialogue extensively. If leaders issue mandates—"This is what we're going to do—period!"—people feel cut out of the loop, disenfranchised. The gears of change are oiled when everyone feels that he or she is doing something with the group. The more listening and talking we do, the more others feel included.

Especially when pastors come into an established church as the new kid on the block, they need to establish strong relationships and open communication lines with the opinion shapers, including the detractors and the doubters. While it is easy to spend time with people who agree with us, most change is thwarted by those who don't agree with us. These are the ones we must work hard to include in our fellowship.

"You've been here a long time," you might say to such individuals. "Would you be willing to meet for lunch every couple of weeks? I'd like your assessment of how I'm tracking with where the church has gone before."

Take notes at these sessions. Nothing stops a critic's mouth like taking him seriously. In later sessions be sure to bring up comments he made weeks ago: "A month ago you said—let's see, your words were: 'You're totally disregarding our traditional values.' I've been working on that. How do you think I'm doing?"

We must discover the cherished values of the old guard. These values can be the springboard for bringing change as we show how the old-guard values call for the changes we advocate. For instance, let's say you are pastoring a traditional, liturgical congregation and you want to introduce a contemporary worship service on Sunday evenings. Instead of the pipe organ and hymns, you hope to have guitars, drums, and worship choruses. A sizable segment of the church resists the change because they fear the loss of the form and ritual and sacraments that are so meaningful to them. "High church" has meaning and value for them in this ever-changing, uncertain world.

You may be tempted simply to keep arguing your point with them—that the church must keep pace with the contemporary world. But your arguments have already swayed everyone they are going to convince. Don't entrench yourself—and your critics. Instead, use their values to make your point: most of the contemporary, fast-paced world knows nothing of the peace and serenity we experience in our liturgy and in the symbolism of the service. We are so blessed by our form of worship that we really owe it to others to introduce them to it. Why don't we start a new church service that will appeal to where such people are now, and then expect that their proximity to us, our church, and our regular service will win them over? Instead of threatening the traditional perspective, you are offering to expose more people to it. The other strategy is to go in and have a massacre and then work with whoever is left—that is, if you're still around. Either way, change is messy. We can deal with mess a little at a time or all at once. You have to make that choice based on your personality.

Dialogue is essential if we are to use opposition to our favor. If we aren't hearing the disagreement, then we aren't hearing. Opposition lets us know what is being said in the congregation and helps us understand any resistance we face. Therefore, I don't try to avoid or clamp down on it. To a degree, I encourage it so that we can discern the issues with which we need to deal. It is ludicrous for me to imagine that a proposed change is right on the first shot.

How we view detractors is crucial to our success at bringing about change. If we take disagreement personally, it degenerates to an us-versus-them situation in which no one wins. Instead of seeing detractors as the opposition, view them as providing constructive criticism. That puts you on the same team. The best leaders maintain the nobility of the process of change.

Be flexible. When we listen to people, we must take what they say seriously. Most ideas can be improved with input. Be willing to modify the *how* in order to accomplish the *what*. Flexibility shows others that we are concerned about their feelings and that we don't insist on having everything our way.

When visiting pastors come to our church, they are invariably struck with the huge number of adults who volunteer in our children's ministry during our two Saturday evening services and two Sunday morning services. We accomplished this goal by being flexible. My goal was to take care of all our children's ministry volunteer needs through our home cell groups (ICUs). I began by convincing the ICU leaders that they could get quality time with the people in their ICUs if they had opportunities to serve together. Since the ICU leaders are supposed to have contact with their people each week, and since we value serving each week in church, wouldn't it be great to do both at one time—serving and contacting the people in their ICUs?

I wanted to assign each ICU to a specific age group of kids for one of the four services. The whole ICU could go to church together and then serve together; there would be more than enough adults in every classroom and a lot of meaningful contact within the ICU. My idea met with lots of resistance: "Every week is too much. There is nothing for all those adults to do in the class. We can't serve all the time." I listened and compromised. Since the apprentice ICU leaders are also supposed to contact the people each week, I offered to let the ICUs divide the children's ministries duties with half the ICU members and the leader coming one week and the other half and the apprentice leader coming the next week. Participants are happy that they only have to serve in children's ministries twice each month, and I feel good that we solved our volunteer needs for the children without having to beg for workers from the pulpit.

Involve others. One truism of change is that when people are included in the planning and implementation of a new idea, they take ownership of it. One of our pastors was scheduled to speak at another church about our cell-group structure, and I asked him to take along a man in our church, whom I'll call Chester, who had resisted the move we had made to spread the pastoral care and nurture responsibilities to our cell-group leaders.

After our pastor finished part of his presentation, he turned to Chester and asked him to talk about his experience with the cell groups. Chester found himself explaining a program with which he didn't fully agree, and then people asked him questions about the very issues that had given him problems. Though Chester had his own reservations, as he "defended" his church before the doubters in the other church, a transformation took place in his heart.

When I saw Chester the next day, he said, "When we began the cell-group structure two years ago, I just wish that we had known what we know now. It would have made things much easier." Actually, Chester had made two years of changes in that two-hour meeting. He illustrates how involvement—even after the fact—can encourage ownership. That is one reason I prefer to implement changes on the periphery rather than making them from the top down.

Experiment. Proposing a change as an experiment lowers the emotional stakes. Let people know that you don't have all the answers, that your program is a prototype, and that adjustments will be made as you go. If the experiment fails, it will be scuttled.

Set a date for assessing the experiment and ask others to debrief with you. Even those who have opposed an idea will start to pull with you if they see positive results. When they are further allowed to give their input about how you might modify and improve the idea, they can begin to buy into it as their own without having to admit how wrong they were or how right you were.

Although calling a proposed change an "experiment" can make it sound iffy and may even doom it to receiving less support from skeptics, an experiment does not require a final vote of approval from everyone. In other words, you can go ahead with a change even before you build consensus. An experiment buys you time. It suspends debate because no one knows what the results will be. Your critics *are waiting* to be able to say, "See, I told you it wouldn't work."

Use the grapevine. One of my favorite methods for introducing change is what I call "leading by rumor." A truthful rumor, spread word of mouth, is a far more effective way to communicate than the church bulletin. People who won't read bulletins or listen to announcements will listen to rumors.

I employed this approach when we added two services on Saturday night. Doubling the number of our services, moving to another day, and adding another Christian education time would be a major undertaking. Not only would we need more volunteer involvement, but we would also face resistance on theological and experiential grounds: The only time you do church is on Sunday morning, right?

Knowing this would be a struggle, I began a rumor. Individually, I told about twenty people that we were toying with the idea of having Saturday evening services. I asked them to pray and think with me about the idea because I knew "not everyone would be able to see the importance and benefit of making this change." I asked them to help me anticipate the sorts of objections *other* people might have.

About a month and a half later, I formally announced the decision in church. By that time, of course, almost everyone had heard about and talked to others about the idea. It was the worst-kept secret in the church. From the moment I began the public presentation about the change, everyone in the sanctuary knew what I was going to announce. I wish I had a videotape of the knowing looks on everyone's face. They were "in the know," on the inside, privy to decisions.

The funny thing about a rumor is that once a person has passed it along, he has a vested interest in the rumor's being true. When he tells someone what is going to happen, he wants it to happen just as he said it would. We never had one peep of opposition to Saturday night services. We made it a nonissue by dealing with it informally by rumor.

Anticipate cultural changes. I will discuss this point in greater detail in chapter 7, but in essence it means to think through how the change you are proposing will bump into unspoken presumptions in the church. For instance, when I proposed that we elect couples (not just men) to our church council, I knew it would raise questions in some people's minds. The questions might not even be raised verbally, but they would be lingering in the back of their minds.

The most obvious question was theological—women "[having] authority over a man" (1 Tim. 2:12). By defining *authority* (the only time this Greek word is used in the Bible) as "acting of oneself; pushing others out of the picture," and stressing that the council is a *group* of people acting *together*, I diffused most of the controversy within our church (I make no attempt to settle the issue theologically for other churches).

The toughest questions were not theological but cultural. Some people in our church had been greatly influenced by the women's movement, and they wanted me to be making a statement that would assert women's rights and free them from male dominance. Others in the church wanted almost the opposite—a reinforcement of the idea that women should either be sent overseas as missionaries (church leaders) or be kept out of decision-making roles here in the United States. If I let the change I was proposing become a pawn in the struggle between those two, equally distorted perspectives, we would miss the point. In anticipation of their likely misinterpretation, I carefully explained what we were doing and why—and what we were not doing. Anticipating what the culture of your church expects will help smooth transitions and change.

Don't try to convince everyone. Twisting people's arms is a sure way to cause conflict. Good ideas that require significant changes are never accepted right away by everyone. Initial opposition by some members is a normal part of the process, so don't fight it. Our church council makes decisions by consensus. If even one council member has reservations about a proposal, he or she can pull the plug on it. I am submitted to our council. Sometimes we wait for months until everyone is in agreement; sometimes we abandon plans because we cannot agree.

But that policy is unrealistic for the entire congregation. On most issues, a unanimous congregational decision is impossible. Once a decision has been formally approved, we tell dissenters,

"It's okay if you don't think this is the right way to go. Perhaps it isn't. But just stick with us, and over time either we'll be convinced you're right or vice versa. And we'll be the better for it." Giving people room to disagree decreases the pressure to get everyone to jump onboard and helps everyone feel a bit more relaxed about change.

Model the change. People who resist changes—for fear of what it will cost them or others—ought to be allowed to see that we are willing to sacrifice along with them. Leaders go first when it comes to sacrifice, last when it comes to privileges. Jesus paid first. For the joy set before him, he endured the cross; he took on himself the likeness of our flesh and became a servant, humbling himself to the point of death.

Often, the most memorable instances of modeling come in little things. For example, when we installed a new parking lot far away from the sanctuary and asked our leaders to park there instead of near the building, it was important for them to see me park there myself. To this day, I have no reserved parking spot; I park where all our leaders park.

Reassure people. Change makes people insecure. *If this is changing,* people think, *other things that are important to me may change. I can't count on this church. Who knows what'll be next?*

If a leader casually dismisses people's fears, he or she loses their trust, so it is crucial to personally reassure people, to let them know we have heard them and are taking their feelings into account. We must reassure people that our relationship with them doesn't depend on whether they go along with this change, that we have a history and a future together. Simply acknowledging that the change is difficult can be a way of assuring people. They worry that they will be shoved aside, forgotten or sacrificed for the sake of the change the leader wants to implement. This is where personal relationship is so vital.

A friend of mine pastors a small church in another country and has expressed grave reservations about some changes that denominational leaders want to implement in that country. Though my friend's opposition expressed itself through several specific arguments, I knew the real issue was the fear that the church would get lost in the process of change. They felt small and all alone. It would have made a great difference if the new denominational leader would have made personal contact with my friend. As an outsider, I commented on what I knew about the new leader—that he was very people-oriented and very sympathetic to the unique struggle of smaller churches. Those reassurances answered what no amount of intellectual argument could answer.

Avoid aspirin. Pain motivates people to welcome change. When all is well, people are complacent. Sometimes the only thing a leader can do about a problem is wait until a congregation's old way of thinking and doing produces such agony that the people can't bear it any longer. That could mean watching a congregation dwindle and finally asking, "Do we want this to keep happening? How many more months should we go without changing?"

The leader's job in such a situation is to accentuate the pain a bit. Take the blinders off people's eyes and bring them face-to-face with reality. The worst thing a leader can do in an ill church is give an aspirin such as "Things look bad, but the Lord is at work in mysterious ways." The leader's job is to keep commenting on the splinter in the foot: "It would be so much better if we took the splinter out. Nothing could be worse than the pain we have now."

Learning to lead is learning to manage change. This truth is borne out in every leader in the Bible, from Moses to Jeremiah, from Jesus to Paul. Our calling as leaders is to be change agents.

Chapter Six

EMPOWERING PEOPLE

The priesthood of every believer was one of the most significant rallying cries of the Great Reformation. The protest against exclusivity in church ministry helped to empower the people of God to do the work of God in their everyday lives. By getting the Scriptures into the hands of the entire church body, reformers took action against the elitist notion that only a qualified few could correctly interpret what God was saying in the Bible.

Since those days, there has been an uneasy distinction between the clergy and the laity: What qualifications of calling, training, and gifting separate the clergy from the laity? What roles are appropriate for one group but not the other? What weaknesses constitute grounds for defrocking a professional priest? And what accomplishments can legitimately lift a layperson to the status of clergy?

These difficult questions have been effectively bypassed by another rallying cry—the cry of our generation: *the ministry of every believer.* Even if that ministry is limited in its scope by a theological perspective about what a layperson cannot do (baptize, serve Communion, and so on), most church leaders today are prepared to acknowledge—even promote—the ministry calling of every believer. The incredible needs that face churches require that most churches mobilize their laity to some level of service involvement.

Even among noncharismatic congregations there is a growing awareness of spiritual gifts and ministries and of ways to identify people's giftings so that they can be slotted into volunteer duties that closely match their ministry orientation. Various theologies have categorized the ministry mixes in the New Testament into "motivational gifts," "equipping ministries," and other categories. No matter how many spiritual gifts church leaders believe are spelled out in the Bible (Is celibacy a spiritual gift? How about hospitality?), almost every pastor accepts the fact that those gifts edify the whole church and ought to be utilized as much as possible.

The Bible is full of promises for our personal recovery from the death our sins have introduced into our lives and promises for our meaningful role in God's grand design to redeem the world. Each believer has a part to play. So significant is that part, that when Jesus comments on the harvest at hand, he urges his disciples to pray for more laborers—not for a miraculous sweep of the Spirit. For his own mysterious purposes, God has chosen to partially link his work on earth to willing human beings with whom he can form a partnership.

IMPOSSIBLE TASKS

Our partnership with God reminds me of an episode with my youngest son, Evan, a few years ago. He had been "discipled" for a couple of weeks by his older brother, Collin, in the meaningful ministry of taking out the trash. This was Evan's first solo day in the ministry, and it happened to be the day the trash cans had to be taken to the curb to be picked up by the garbagemen.

Evan managed to get all the trash out to the cans, but the cans themselves were too heavy for his eight-year-old muscles. He couldn't get the cans to the curb. I had given him a chore that he couldn't do without me. As serious and intent as he was about his job, when we lugged the cans out to the curb, most of the actual lifting and carrying was done by me, his father. I could have moved the cans without him, but I couldn't have empowered him with significance without his participation—meager as it was. When we finally realize that God's assignments in our life are meant more to bond us with him than they are to do something for him we will grasp the point of effective church leadership.

Our job as leaders is not to accomplish tasks, quotas, or logistical goals. Churches don't produce anything if they do not produce transformed people. The jobs that need doing, the needs that need meeting, the problems that need solving—none of these are the real point of church. What we use to face those challenges is the point. Will the challenges become opportunities to empower people with significance, or will they degenerate into back-breaking straws that overload our already overwhelmed schedule as leaders? Will we do everything or empower everyone?

PROCESS OF DEVELOPMENT

The development of people over time brings us back to church as a process—not a continuous series of one problem or need after another, but a process of developing individual believers into resourceful ministers (servers), each of whom contributes out of the giftedness and equipping of his or her life. The church body becomes linked by the association, companionship, and instrumentality of the members. This is the message of Ephesians 4:11–16.

When the people of a church have been trained and discipled in their unique gift mix, they are more *efficient* (using less personal energy) and *effective* (getting more done) than if everyone is trained generically. Certainly a great deal of what people need to learn in the kingdom can and should be taught in large group settings. Foundational doctrines, scriptural truths, points of wisdom, and basic understandings are better communicated in the public forum. But empowering people also must involve one-on-one ministry and the unique shaping that every saint needs to understand his or her individual ministry calling. Sometimes it is as simple as helping people see what is true about them.

A man in our church—I'll call him Toby—went through a time of tremendous insecurity and doubt about his beliefs. He even wondered about his place in the church. Question after question troubled his mind. After I preached, Toby would often approach me with a worried look on his face and say something to this effect: "I hear what you're saying, Pastor, but what about . . .?" He saw the tensions of truth in issues like grace and law, God's sovereignty and man's freedom. He struggled with the big and small difficulties of interpreting Scripture: "But doesn't it also say . . .?" As a result, he felt that something was wrong with him, that he had a faulty faith. He doubted his sincerity, his character, and his future.

What Toby saw as a weakness in himself, I saw as the fledgling gift of teaching. Teachers are bothered by the little things that don't trouble most others. They want to understand everything, both to satisfy their own curiosity and to draw upon for the sake of instructing others. None of Toby's questions were belligerent or argumentative. They didn't come from an angry spirit or a bitter heart. They weren't even that confused. They were just hard to answer with brief statements. They were thoughtful, so they required thought to answer. One day I assured him, "You are fine. You are a teacher. You'll figure it out. What troubles you teacher-type people always ends up comforting those you will teach in the future."

At that point in his life, Toby had never formally taught anything in church, and my words were something of a revelation to him. They helped him accept himself, and eventually he found a place to express that teaching gift fruitfully in our church. He doesn't have a title, but he functions as a man who grasps difficult issues and then translates them in a way that makes them easily accepted by others.

Another teacher in our church loves to act out lessons for the children's assemblies. He is incredibly gifted with using analogies. After almost every service, he shares a thought or two with me about something I said in the sermon. I'm glad he attends the first of our four weekend services, because I often use his thoughts in the other three.

SIGNIFICANT AFFIRMATION

Leadership is essentially a human business—especially in the church. Church leadership is the one-on-one task of helping individually gifted and called people find their unique purpose in the kingdom of God. The leader's responsibility is to empower God's people to serve "according to the proper working of each individual part" (Eph. 4:16 NASB). That is no small task. Most churches have considerable trouble just getting enough volunteers. Pastors plead from the pulpit for nursery workers, youth group chaperones, and office helpers. Most churches also suffer a chronic shortage of quality leaders. For the work of ministry, the people in the pews can seem feeble, ill-matched, uncertain, unmotivated. Just how do we empower the saints for the work of the ministry?

Perhaps the greatest gift a leader can give a follower is the gift of significance. As we discussed in chapter 2, the weighty role a leader has in a person's life is best used to affirm and commend that person. Self-esteem is an oxymoron. No matter how much a person with low self-esteem tries to think well of himself, since he doesn't value himself, he doesn't value his opinion; so his opinion about himself doesn't count for anything. Only those we esteem can build our self-esteem. When we value a leader's opinion, that opinion about us will stand the assault of our own low opinion. Church leaders—more so than any other leaders—ought to recognize how desperately downtrodden people are who have been raised in families where there is no affirmation or who hold jobs that do little to fulfill them. People need affirmation.

Affirmation is not flattery. It is not a sugarcoated series of lies spoken just to make a miserable failure less miserable. Affirmation is kingdom stuff. When we first arrive in heaven, the words we have most wanted to hear since getting saved will be spoken: "I love you. Well done. . . ." If that declaration from God will greet us at the end of our life and ministry, shouldn't pastors and church leaders—who are trying to prepare people for that day—be saying similar things along the way?

Somewhere the church adopted a strange idea that people are more prone to conceit than to low self-esteem. My observations have led me to believe just the opposite: while 10 percent struggle with too high an opinion of themselves, 90 percent find it nearly impossible to think that they are worth much of anything. They believe, "If I cannot be worth much, I cannot do much of worth." People desperately need encouragement, upbuilding, and consolation. In the popular book *The One-Minute Manager*, Blanchard and Johnson say, "People who feel good about themselves produce good results."[1]

Leaders should not be putting maple syrup on burned waffles. Leaders with integrity will risk disfavor by telling their followers when something is wrong with their life choices or with their ministry activity. But most of the time, neither the people nor what they are doing in ministry is wrong. Usually their efforts are sincere and helpful. And our encouragement to them will give them courage to face the daunting tasks ahead. Most people are reluctant to aim high or go through change because they are afraid of failing or losing. Good leaders know how to instill courage in their followers.

Second Chronicles 32:6–8 and passages like it are probably not highlighted in many pastors' Bibles, yet it is one of many texts that attests to the uplifting power of a leader's words. The Assyrian king had arrayed a vast host against the people of God, but "Hezekiah encouraged them with these words: 'Be strong and courageous. Do not be afraid or discouraged. . . .' And the people gained confidence from what Hezekiah the king of Judah said." What a marvelous portrayal of the crucial role—indeed, sometimes the deciding factor—a leader's inspiring words can have. We lead churches largely populated by people who feel like those Israelites in Jerusalem: paralyzed, uncertain, dispirited by what faces them. They have been battered, abused, and intimidated, and they desperately want and need someone to inspire them.

Nehemiah serves as another biblical model of an empowering and inspirational leader. Sanballat and the other enemies of God's people had conspired to mock, demoralize, and intimidate the workers who were rebuilding the walls of Jerusalem. Those workers, like our church volunteers, felt their strength failing. When Nehemiah saw the fear in them, he arose and said, "Do not be afraid of them; remember the Lord who is great and awesome, and fight for your brothers, your sons, your daughters, your wives, and your houses" (Neh. 4:14 NASB). Nehemiah translated the numeric and military realities of the looming battle into terms of true significance: "The battle isn't about what may happen to us; it is about what will happen for others." The people had an opportunity to do for others what those others could not do for themselves. True significance—a meaningful reason to lay down your life—can be found only by doing things for the sake of others.

ASSUMPTIONS THAT EMPOWER

As we consider how to "stimulate one another to love and good deeds" (the biblical phrase for *empower*), we should remember a point that we have come to again and again in this book. *How* we think about something ends up shaping *what* we think and do. The most important factor in empowering people is our assumptions. While management literature abounds with principles for effective delegation (I will list some later in the chapter) those principles are lame without the following three assumptions:

1. *The best person for a job is someone not yet totally qualified.* Last year I delegated responsibility for our annual men's retreat to one of my associate pastors. I attend our men's meetings, but I let other staff and volunteers lead them. Our speaker was a well-known pastor from southern California, and on the first night he harpooned us, impaling us to the backs of our chairs with a great message.

My associate pastor was acting as the host for the evening, so it was his job to conclude the service. Sitting in back, I thought, *Following a good speaker is tough. I wonder how Donny will wrap this up?*

Because the teaching had been so powerful and convicting, the room was silent. Donny stepped shyly to the platform, took the mike, and stammered, "Well, we're going to have dessert now. The food is off here to the side. That teaching was, uh, a great dessert for our hearts; now let's get one for our stomachs."

No, Donny, I thought, *that's not the way to do it.*

After the men cleared out to get their desserts, I meandered up to Donny and asked, "So how did you like following a great speaker?"

"It was terrible," he admitted. "For the last ten minutes of his message, I flipped through my Bible trying to find something meaningful to say. I just didn't know what to do."

"Can we agree that his message was a little more than a *dessert?*" I asked.

"Oh, yeah, it was a great message."

I gently explained what had happened: "Do you see what you did? You deflected the impact of the teaching by immediately talking about logistics for dessert. In the future, when you follow a speaker, your role is to validate the message. To whatever extent you acknowledge the message, you are telling everyone to buy into it. If you trivialize or dismiss it, then the congregation will, as well. Acknowledge some point of conviction that the message brought to your heart. That frees others to recognize the conviction God has brought to their hearts. Respond to what was spoken, and do it personally."

Donny received my advice with a great spirit.

Later while talking with the guest speaker, I asked, "How did you like the follow-up to your message by my associate? Pretty lousy, huh?"

"Frankly, it was pretty bad," he agreed.

"Isn't that great?" I replied.

"What do you mean?"

"Here's a man who didn't know how to follow a great speaker; because of this traumatic experience of trying to follow you, he is eager for help. I bet Donny will follow speakers better than anybody in this church for the rest of his life."

The speaker got a sad look of realization in his eyes. "Our church back home is too big to do what you do. We can't let people get trained at our expense."

Churches can reach a size where they cannot afford mistakes because the repercussions are too great. That doesn't make them bad churches, but if they want to keep developing people as they did when they were smaller congregations, they have to find smaller settings to give people a chance to fail. Real ministry creates an ongoing string of teachable moments. That's why the person most qualified for a job is an unqualified person who has shown potential and a teachable spirit.

We have chosen to be a church that empowers people by giving them a chance to blow it. When people are given that chance, they have a chance to succeed wonderfully. After they succeed, they tend to become long-term contributors to the whole church process.

2. *The real work of ministry is not getting the work done, but getting the people done.* Perfected (completed) people are more important than perfect (flawless) programs. An event mentality of church stresses the quality of the events—Christmas banquets, marriage seminars, choir performances, mission presentations, and so on. A process mentality church, on the other hand, keeps focusing on the people who will "put on" those events more than on the people who will "come to" those events.

I am not arguing for poor performances, lousy seminars, or ill-prepared events. That is part of the trap in most leaders' assumptions; they presume that quality events can only be produced by *already qualified* people. That assumption is only true if these hidden assumptions are also true: (1) There is not enough time for the unqualified to learn what they need to know; (2) there is no one available to teach the unqualified what they need to know; (3) there is no plan to do anything more in the future than what the church is doing now.

The reality in most churches is not a lack of willing volunteers but a lack of thoughtfulness and planning on the part of the leaders. People can become qualified if they are given time and teaching. That is the premise upon which pastors prepare their sermons; they develop their congregants by teaching them what they need to know to live a successful Christian life. Shouldn't we be able to employ the same process for events and programs?

As a church, we base most of what we do on the idea that you ought to have an apprentice with you learning how you do what you do. The children's Christmas choir director keeps her eye out for a parent who has the obvious interest in and musical skills for becoming the next director in a year or two. Mission teams led by a pastor are as much about discipling future lay team leaders as they are about ministering in another culture.

The more exciting or frightening the event, the more willing the participants are to accept instruction in preparation for the event. Our mission teams, for instance, meet for two to three months prior to their departure date—every week for three hours—to review foundational truths such as personal devotions, accountability, and servanthood. We ask team members to be prepared with their life testimony and two brief teachings from Scripture. When we tell the team members that they might be called upon to share in a church unexpectedly, they are willing to study and prepare.

Good and bad attitudes tend to pop to the surface when people feel a bit insecure and responsible for things. A layman named Dennis wrote me a note after recently becoming a cell-group leader. He said: "I never thought I could lead a group and teach. But as I have been praying, God has really amazed me." Included with his note were two articles from the secular press about how employees of many Silicon Valley companies meet for daily or weekly prayer groups. He was telling me that he prays about his cell group just as those employees pray about their work. Imagine what is going on in his life that would not be happening if he merely attended a meeting put on by an already qualified person.

The real work of ministry is not getting the work done; it is using the work to get people done. Performance is secondary. Every event and activity of our church is an opportunity to get our discipling, training hands on a human being. Granted, this means that we have more messes to clean up. Proverbs 14:4 says, "Where there are no oxen, the manger is empty [that is, clean], but from the strength of an ox comes an abundant harvest." As mentioned in chapter 1, if we want to have a neat, perfect program, we can, but we won't have much harvest. On the other hand, if we are willing to wear rubber boots and carry a shovel, much can happen.

Let's not forget that all this empowerment is a process, too. We didn't randomly select Dennis to be a cell-group leader six weeks after he was saved. He had been discipled and observed by his cell-group leader for many months. Jesus was quite clear about the process for selecting people to put in charge of your church's most important activities: those who are faithful in little things are to be put in charge of greater things.

An event-oriented church tends not to have many small things over which people can be put in charge. The few people in such churches who have been validated to be leaders are so busy with all that they are doing, that they don't have time to delegate responsibility. They know that it often takes more time to teach a job to someone else than it does to do the job themselves. Instead of giving responsibility, they pass out assignments. But until someone has been given responsibility, we cannot really know if he or she is faithful.

This cycle of the "busy few" works against the necessary process of watching and validating people over time. Giving people tasks in church in order to empower them is a completely different mind-set from giving people tasks to get performance out of them. Delegating jobs with performance uppermost in mind actually frustrates empowerment. One of two things can happen: (1) Someone is delegated a huge task, and when she fails, the leader blames her and vows never to delegate again. The reason she failed, though, is that the leader didn't spend enough time cultivating her abilities or watching how she performed at little things before giving her a greater task. (2) Someone is delegated a huge task, and she succeeds. The pastor then thinks, *I have my worker. I'll never have to find someone to do the Christmas banquet again.* Regrettably, that volunteer will never have the opportunity to progress beyond the Christmas banquet because she did so well at it. She is stuck with the job until Jesus comes. And no one else will have the opportunity to be shaped by the process of learning how to do the banquet. Thus, our highest goal should be empowerment, not performance.

3. *Leaders are made.* Few things are more of an indictment of a leader's performance than his or her plea for more leaders. The complaint that there just aren't enough potential leaders in our congregations points to a failure on our part. Leadership development, raising people to a level they couldn't reach on their own, is our job.

The problem comes when we have an image in mind of what a leader should be. We put that picture under the chins of church members, decide that they don't match, and presume that heaven hasn't sent us the leaders we need. But leaders are developed, not sent ready-made from heaven. Nor are they formed in our prayer closet (though prayer is important). Leaders take shape through the ongoing investment of our lives in others.

The misapplication of several Scriptures can aggravate a leadership shortage. For instance, how we teach about the equipping gifts described in Ephesians 4:11 can lead to an unintentional elitism. We can convey the notion that some have these exalted gifts and the rest don't. People catch on to this idea. The average guy sitting in church hears about the equippers—evangelists, pastor-teachers, prophets, apostles—and thinks, *I'm certainly not one of those,* because he can't see himself up front behind a pulpit. He presumes he is always supposed to be one of those people being equipped; he will never be a leader. But the equippers are not the only leaders in the body of Christ, perhaps not even the majority.

Another example of a sometimes misapplied Scripture passage is Jesus' parable of the talents. Some people believe that some are born as five-talent Christians, some as three-talent Christians, and the vast majority as one-talent folks destined only to help leaders do their glorious work, as though God magnificently equips a few and to the rest says, "Well, what can I say?"

That is not the heart of God. He takes nine months to intricately weave the particulars of our being in the womb. He doesn't do that to make a mediocre person. Every creation of God is magnificent. Moreover, as I have already said, Scripture teaches that if we are faithful in little, God makes us masters of much. To relegate people to a lower strata of Christendom is a horrible injustice.

A fatalistic mind-set about leadership causes us to hunt only for five-talent Christians instead of fully developing every person God puts into our charge. If many people in our church are still one-talent believers, could part of the reason be that we have not given them opportunities for leadership that match their faithfulness?

Leadership isn't a rare skill found only at the top of an organization. Leaders and followers aren't like oil and water, with leaders always rising to the surface. The body of Christ is more like vegetable stew. Every person is a pinch of spice adding flavor to the mix. Remove even one pinch of spice, and the whole stew suffers.

MOTIVATION

Motivation must precede delegation. Churches with a high percentage of attendees involved long-term in volunteer ministry have leaders who don't just manage—they inspire. Inspirational leaders don't demand or coerce, don't heap on guilt or put sole emphasis on duty. They motivate in positive ways, such as the following.

Be enthusiastic about the future. God always has plans to give us a future filled with blessing. The new covenant is all about the future, and it speaks to us about what we can become, not about what we have been. God's Word is his promise. It all points to our tomorrow and what we should do today to avail ourselves of that future. If our past alone prescribes our future, then all is lost. But if God—who changes the seasons and works his purposes through frail people like us—is running things, then there is always hope.

Pastors who are not enthusiastic and positive about the future are missing one of the most critical truths in the universe.

Perhaps that is because they have forgotten another great truth: The difference between our past and our future is repentance. Repentance is the beginning of the Good News. Without repentance there is no conversion; without conversion, everything remains the same.

Energy and optimism are contagious. Christians must not base their faith on emotion, but that doesn't mean that we are to be comatose. If leaders downplay feelings, those who desperately need "oomph" receive little input from the very people to whom they are looking for inspiration. People's feelings are real even if they are not accurate. Rather than trying to pep-talk people out of their discouragement, it may be more effective to acknowledge the reality of what they feel. Jesus was touched with our feelings of despair, loneliness, and fear, but he knew that God had a future for him and for us.

What it means to be strong in God came back to me during a recent season of trial in my life and in the life of our whole church. At every point it seemed as though the enemy was scoring victory after victory. The situation was way beyond remedy by verbal Band-Aids offered by well-meaning saints: "I'm sure it will all work out." *Maybe it will*, I thought, *but will I be around when it does*?

I wasn't feeling strong. In fact, quite the opposite was true. But then I realized that I still believed three things: God is good; God is great; and his Word is true. Though I could not be enthusiastic about my present, and I told the people so, I could remain enthusiastic about what the Word of a great, good God told me. We had a future!

Be dedicated to the mission. In the long run, it won't be the dynamics or the charisma of a leader's personality that empowers people. They may be attracted by the giftedness and the qualities of the leader's public persona, but that is show business, not kingdom enablement.

By "being dedicated", I do not mean the sort of private martyrdom some leaders make themselves suffer—working long, thankless hours alone, bearing the weight of the whole ministry.

Dedication does involve sacrifice and labor, but it is more of a mentality and a disposition than it is an activity. I like to think of dedication as what I am doing with my life. If I am dedicated to loving, mending, training, and sending people, then I can ask the people in my congregation to *join me* in doing likewise. A "commitment to excellence," a chance to "three-peat" a national title, a call to "be the best you can be" are all examples of someone's dedication that can be joined by others. The people in our churches will be inspired by that to which we truly give our lives. We can say to them, "Help me make this church a place that will really ..."

Care about and believe in people. People are inspired by how leaders treat them and feel about them, which in turn affects their outlook toward the work of the Lord and their part in that work. Inspirational leaders convey sincere warmth, concern, and interest.

A cordial relationship between leaders and followers—the kind that communicates respect and welcome—will keep both the leaders and the followers going even when other circumstances are discouraging. Affection, regard, love, and attachment are the essence of agape love. God's love wants to have us near to him. His love delights in us.

People do not trust leaders who do not care. Much of the attachment and loyalty people feel toward their leaders has to do with a desire to be together in the future. People may be temporarily blinded by a leader's charisma and by their desire to have a future with such a leader, but as soon as they come to realize that the leader has no desire to be with them, those people will not remain inspired.

We inspire people by believing in them more than they believe in themselves. Every leader wants talented and gifted followers. Because people usually cannot see their own giftedness, they presume that their leaders are not that interested in having them around in the future. Wise leadership keeps seeing and believing what people could become if they are obedient and discipled. The intrinsic qualities they have are probably still "in the rough" and need cutting and polishing. When a leader glimpses those qualities, people can sense it.

We have just promoted two couples in our church to a newly designated role of "laypastor." I'm pleased with the term because it confuses the demarcation between layperson and clergy. When I called one of the couples to tell them our plan, the wife insisted on knowing what it was that I "saw" in them that qualified them. I only had to bring up an example that she used earlier in the conversation: having just provided marriage counseling to one of our staff pastors, they felt very close to that pastoral couple and wanted to remain under their care. "See," I said, "what other pastors trust about you is what I have known about you."

Some people in our church got together to give my wife and me a very nice surprise gift. The card that accompanied the gift was more meaningful to me than the gift itself. The card said, "You believed in us when no one else did."

Develop others' self-regard. Although for several decades people in our society have been patting themselves on the back and telling themselves they're fine, they don't believe it. They need leaders whom they respect, whose opinion they value, to affirm their worth and abilities. People feel good about following leaders who build their self-regard. One way we build a person's self-regard is by recognizing his or her uniqueness.

I was talking with some of the female leaders in our church, and I thought it would encourage them to know how each had a unique ability to discern things in the lives of others. I used several metaphors to explain what I meant. One woman could pick up a twig from the ground and, based on its details, understand everything going on in the surrounding area. The second woman was like a smart missile; she honed in on the critical issue or problem in any situation. Another woman had loving discernment. She'd smile, love on you, and kindly say, "I'm sorry, but you're wrong." The last woman I described was like a pack of hunting dogs who could chase an issue up a tree and bark until others came to take care of it. We had lots of fun with those metaphors. People need mirrors in their lives. I was privileged to hold such a mirror up to these women so they could see themselves. They were encouraged to know that they were known.

Catch people doing things well. Be more cheerleader than critic—not "Rah! Rah!" zany and wild, but let people know how much you appreciate who they are and what they do. Leaders need to say things like, "I've been watching you, and if you keep making the kind of progress you have been, there's no telling what will happen to you three months or three years from now." Encouragement doesn't mean hype or a con job—telling people who aren't doing well that they are—but rather opening people's eyes to the glory God puts in each of his children. When that gifting leads them to do things well, we must tell them so.

When I coach soccer, I usually start the season with a team meeting for the parents to let them get to know me, my philosophy of coaching, and some of my expectations of them as parents. Invariably I make the point that I will not allow parents to yell critical or discouraging comments *even at their own children* during the game. I say something like, "Let's all try to catch the kids doing something they are supposed to be doing. Besides, we probably couldn't do any better than they are doing. The sidelines don't afford the same perspective as on the field." People in church, like kids on a soccer field, do better when their confidence is bolstered.

Offer stimulating involvement. We need to place people in the kind of work that inspires them. Researchers have discovered four things people want from their work:

1. *To succeed at a challenging task.* Accomplishing something simple isn't enough. People want to take on something that tests them. They want to prevail against the odds. The job must stretch them but not so much that no amount of effort, training, or persistence will bring success.

2. *To be part of something larger than themselves.* They want to belong to something bigger in scope and duration than themselves. They want to contribute to a cause that will outlast themselves.

3. *To do something well.* People want to produce excellence, to take pride in what they do. Not everyone is an artist or a good manager of details, but within the personal capabilities each person possesses, he wants to do well at what he's doing.

4. *To make a difference.* They want their contribution to count for something in the world.

The church can offer people an unparalleled opportunity for stimulating, meaningful involvement. If people are not volunteering, one of three things may be true: they've been inadvertently trained by the church not to want these things; they've been wounded in their souls; or they've lost hope. If they have been trained to expect trivial work in church, they can be retrained by a trusting leader for important tasks. If they are wounded, a loving leader can heal them. If they are hopeless, a faith-filled leader can restore their confidence in the future.

Focus on the positive. Keep your eyes on what the group is becoming rather than on what it isn't being now. This is a way to welcome the future that God has in mind for you. For instance, I'm in the process of trying to orient our congregation more toward evangelism—a task that will probably never be finished. But instead of berating the congregation with phrases like "We need to be more open to opportunities to witness," I try to talk about developments, stories, or thoughts within the congregation that point in the direction we are headed.

A few weeks ago I told the church that I had become "Mr. Chatty." I was having the almost uncontrollable urge to speak to everyone I met—in elevators, at the gas station, in the market. I said to the church, "Becoming accustomed to that kind of easy familiarity with people is one of the surest signs that God is opening up opportunities to witness."

Inspiration is vital, but we can't stop there. Some leaders can motivate people to run through walls, but they lack the skills to plug them in and train them for the task. Inspiration without mobilization leads to frustration.

MOBILIZATION

Mobilization means recruiting the right person for the job, equipping that person for the task, and releasing him or her to serve in meaningful ways. Most churches have a desperate time trying to get people to volunteer. No matter how many attend the church, there never seem to be enough workers. But there is a solution, and it has two parts.

First, hold your leaders responsible for mobilizing. Begin with any quality leaders you have (which in many churches will be just one or two). At The Coastlands we evaluate the effectiveness of leaders primarily on the basis of how many others they can mobilize to do the job, not on how well they do it themselves.

Second, if leaders have trouble getting volunteers, explain why. People generally don't volunteer out of grand altruism; they volunteer because of a relationship with the person who asks for help. To the degree that leaders pour their lives into developing others, others will say yes when asked to volunteer.

One motto at The Coastlands is "Never do alone what you can do with another person." Why waste work on yourself? Getting a job done is less important than getting people done. Every task should be a platform for discipleship.

My staff knows if they complain, "I can't get anyone to do such and such," I translate it into a confession: "I have to confess that I've been so busy with other things that I haven't made it a priority to invest my life in people. I've been living an isolated life, so busy with what I'm doing that no one feels any obligation to me for what I've done in his or her life."

For leaders to say they can't get volunteers is the ultimate admission of failure. It says more about the leadership than about the congregation. Leadership as a process releases other people and empowers them to act meaningfully in ways that will benefit and enhance the work of the whole church. The easiest way to empower people is to share information and authority.

Our church leadership structures should be built on information and communication, not around hierarchy. The industrial smokestack model of the authority chain simply won't work in a volunteer organization like a church, in which so much value is placed on relationship and servanthood. People feel empowered when they receive information that is not known to everyone. This is the idea behind the "mysteries" in the New Testament. The mystery is not mysterious to those with whom it has been shared. It is only mysterious to those on the outside. Generally speaking, the church world has this down well when it comes to theology. Pastors are eager to share information in their sermons, but not too willing to reveal things about finances, decisions, and future plans for the church. Doesn't it seem odd that leaders will talk freely about the "mystery of the age," but not about the staff position they hope to open up next fall?

Equipping people for ministry goes way beyond teaching them Bible lessons. Historically, the church has presumed that if it is teaching (informing), it is empowering. But it isn't. Along with giving people what they need to know in order to do what they need that knowledge to do, we must also give them an opportunity to use what they have been taught. They must use what they learn. Hands-on implementation is equally important as information in the empowerment process.

A pastor friend from Australia phoned me to talk about a new leadership class his church was conducting. "We've graduated two groups of leaders," he said with great satisfaction.

"That's great!" I exclaimed. "So what are your graduates doing now? I trust you had a specific role in mind for them as they went through the training."

"Oh, no, no," he said. "We just train them."

"Your people aren't dumb," I replied. "How long will it be until they realize the leadership training is a joke? They aren't training to do anything; they're training to come back and get more training: leadership training level one, level two, level three, level four...."

Holding training sessions is much easier than figuring out how to use trainees. That's why we're so good at dispensing information. But until we have decided where to put the graduates, we have no business training them.

A pastor who gives people information and opportunity still needs to give them permission. Too often we give someone a job but put them on a short leash. We don't release them to act in significant ways. Sure, they probably won't do their work right for a while, but when we have the assumption that church is a process, we don't care whether they get it right at first as long as they keep at it. We train them a little at a time, over time. The more authority and decision-making opportunities we give staff and volunteers, the more effective our organization will become.

Our church was planning to install a kitchen. A woman in the church, named Sandy, who enjoys research, went to the county planning office and checked into various building codes and requirements. When the time came for the church to make decisions about the kitchen, it was Sandy, not I, providing leadership. She was the authority, and that's the way I wanted it.

One man in our church has the gift of giving, but he was down on himself for what he thought was a lack of spirituality. "Don't you realize you're a giver?" I asked. "Just as God gives me a message to speak each week, so he gives you resources to give. Both are equally spiritual." That released him. Since then he has found contentment in giving. I tell him things about our financial situation as a church that I do not share with many people other than our church council. I'm not trying to get him to give—he already does that generously. I'm simply wanting to reinforce my sense of his trustworthiness in money matters. I let him advise me or pray for me or whatever he wants to do when I give him the information.

Let people know they're needed. Sometimes we inspire others to tackle a job, give them adequate training, but then forget about them. We take them for granted.

I was with two wonderful guys in our church. "You know what?" I said. "We're all we have."

They gave me a *What do you mean?* look.

"Perhaps the day will come when we'll have more money, more people, and more giftedness, but that day isn't here. We're all we have. But I'm convinced right now that we're all we need. I know you're already a significant part of the church, and I just want to invite you again to join me in accomplishing something for the kingdom of God. I need you. Will you help me?"

I wasn't trying to recruit them for a particular task at that moment, and my comment certainly wasn't meant as an insult. I was affirming that we're in the church together. Every great purpose we have in the work of the kingdom ought to make great people in the process. If we accomplish great things, but no one grows in the process, we have fallen short. If we make great people but accomplish nothing else, we also have fallen short. We need both. Ultimately the quality of a leader's work is discerned by the quality of his or her followers and the nobility of what the leader and the followers were able to accomplish together.

Chapter Seven

ADJUSTING CULTURE

Our study of leadership has been based on the understanding that the intangible, immaterial elements of church are far more influential in shaping the entire church environment than are the types of activities normally focused on by pastors. While the more traditional elements of program, staffing, and facilities do have their place in any serious examination of what makes churches successful, the invisible aspects of church offer us more promise because they are actually much easier to change than the physical ones.

By their very nature, spiritual matters tend to be intangible. Intangible *spiritual* ingredients for a vital church, such as prayer, teaching, and faith, do not depend on wealth, planning commissions, or numerous associate pastors to vastly improve. We can do something about them almost as soon as we see the need.

Seeing church as a process enables church leaders to have a meaningful and informed way to also work on the intangible *organic* components of their congregation no matter what its current size, wealth, or structure. Leaders who see the need for change can move ahead with few hindrances.

In this chapter we will be looking at one of the least tangible but most important of all the *organic* components of a church: its culture. Every congregation, like every person, has a personality distinct from every other. The *personality* of a church can be seen in its attitudes, beliefs, priorities, assumptions, values, budgets, schedules, and relationship networks. The dynamics that make up a church's personality are a complex combination of attributes we call *church culture*. An effective leader must be familiar with the church culture and know how to work with it—indeed, when to change it in order to keep leading where God is going.

ELEMENTS OF AN ORGANIZATION'S CULTURE

Every church is a unique collection of people whom God sets in the body as he wills. Therefore, every church has a unique perspective on how to do church: what it means to be committed, how politically involved the congregation should be (and with which issues), what to do with the budget (how much goes to missions as opposed to the homeless), how to make decisions as a congregation, what style of music to greet parishioners with each week, how much individual expression to encourage in corporate worship, what type of counseling to provide, what type of teaching to use, and so on. The unique mix of perspectives on hundreds of such issues makes up a collective paradigm, an organizational mind-set, a group personality—a church culture.

Church culture as I am defining it is not ethnic or socioeconomic per se. It is not the difference between Swedes and Jamaicans, though nationality will obviously affect a church culture. Church culture is the difference between congregations—congregations that can be in the same neighborhood, of the same denomination, ministering to people with the same socioeconomic and ethnic characteristics, and with pastors of the same age, yet despite such similarities, have different cultures.

Edgar Schein aptly says that culture in an organization is "a pattern of basic assumptions—invented, discovered, or developed by a given group as it learns to cope with its problems . . . that has worked well enough to be considered valid and, therefore, to be taught to new members as the correct way to perceive, think, and feel in relation to those problems."[1]

Churches and the people in them are always confronted by problems—spiritual, relational, financial, and physical. We have needs and crises. Tom broke his pelvis in a fall at work, and his family could sure use dinners for two weeks to make the blow to the family less traumatic; the worship team needs a soprano; an abusive former husband of one of the new converts is threatening to charge the youth pastor with kidnapping because he took one of the kids out after school at the mother's request but without the dad's permission; a new staff member is learning to acknowledge that he shouldn't try doing everything himself; the rest rooms need painting; the leadership base is departing more rapidly than we can develop new leaders; and summer has brought a severe drop in attendance and income. Sound familiar? Though we spend a lot of time praying and hoping that after the next hurdle we won't be faced with any more crises, most leaders have come to acknowledge that there is no escaping trouble in a broken world.

As time goes along, churches confront one difficulty after another and resolve sad, sticky, or tough situations. The ways that the collective church deals with those problems becomes a significant part of who they are as a church and how they perceive themselves, their world, and their assignment. It doesn't happen all at once. Slowly, accidentally, by trial and error, a congregational personality takes shape much as a human personality does.

A pioneer church, for instance, may resolve its need for a building in one of several ways. It may decide that purchasing a smaller place is better than leasing a larger one—permanence is preferable to flexibility. Or if it is forced to set up and tear down equipment every Sunday, it can try to make this easier on the congregation by asking for set-up volunteers to work one month in four (thereby lessening the load), or it can celebrate the privilege of such behind-the-scenes labor (thereby giving the work significance).

Some churches hire child-care workers for special events like a worship night; others require that the worship team divide in two and alternate between serving in the ensemble and serving in the nursery. Opposition from city hall leads one church to mount a prayer and petition crusade; it leads another church to "dig a well" someplace else. City hall can be a fact of life, an instrument of the devil or of the hand of God—all depending on how a church interprets things.

People's counseling needs are addressed by staff counselors with psychological credentials at one church and by lay counselors who move in discernment and deliverance at another church. Evangelism is confined to participation in city-wide crusades at one church and is completely unstructured and unmentioned at another. Discipleship is stressed above academic instruction at one church, while social activism is highlighted above cell-group ministry at another church. These are nuances of church culture.

How do we minister to single moms; screen potential molesters from children's ministry; answer requests for money or shelter from street people; give a firm foundation to new converts; promote missions; educate voters to moral implications in upcoming elections; balance the tensions of couples in the church going through a divorce; take care of children of parents who attend two services; distance ourselves from (or identify with) Christian causes or spiritual streams; balance outreach to lost teens and inreach to our own disaffected youngsters? With each issue addressed, a church develops its own flavor and distinctive—its own culture. But church culture is not just a product of facing problems. It can develop in any number of ways, eventually showing itself as the givens, the assumptions, the way a church thinks about and does things. Most of those assumptions are unwritten; they are not usually visible enough to be codified into policy statements or position papers. But they do exist.

To help you identify the various aspects of your church culture, let's look at the six elements of church culture where the differences between churches will be most clearly seen:

1. *Common history.* These are the events, people, and experiences that have been melded together over a fairly long period of time. They are only selectively remembered as isolated occurrences, but as they are transmitted over time, they communicate the church's core values and beliefs. Few details of long-ago events are remembered, but like illustrations in a sermon, what *is* remembered makes a point and communicates a message.

For instance, how people at The Coastlands view evangelism is less a consequence of my teaching and more a consequence of the experiences we had when we started the church. Since we could only rent our facility on Sunday mornings and for the rest of the week had nothing else we could do "at church," we had a lot of Trivial Pursuit parties, pizza feasts, and spaghetti dinners. We went from one house to another inviting friends, neighbors, and people we met at the grocery store. We had fun, and people who didn't know the Lord would say what a great time they were having.

"You think this is fun," we'd say, "you ought to come on Sunday morning."

"Really? What are you doing?"

"Church."

"Okay, I'll give it a try."

Many came and dedicated their lives to following Christ. Consequently, our definition of evangelism evolved over time into simply introducing your old friends to your new friends.

Another of the core values at The Coastlands is the mentality of "coming to go." In other words, the whole point of receiving training is what we will eventually be called upon to do with it for the sake of others. "Coming to go" is not just the result of intentional instruction. It also comes from the fact that our church was pioneered by a team who left the comfort of their church to bring that comfort to others. With each of our fourteen church plantings through the years, our church culture has become more and more attuned to the "going" mentality.

People affected by the church culture cannot always explain why they think as they do—except to attribute it to the pastor's teaching. For example, when Gary and Bonny, my associate pastors, announced their intention to pioneer a church in Nashville, Tennessee, twelve to fifteen families gave strong consideration to moving from California just to be a part of the church plant.

Over and over I heard people say something close to what one man told me at breakfast last week: "My wife and I are thinking about moving to Nashville."

"Really? I didn't know you were that close to Gary and Bonny. Do you really think you are going to go for it?"

"We're not that close to them personally. *But it's like you always say:* we should be open to the possibility of going somewhere someday."

Our church culture has accumulated and assimilated the stories of the many groups of people who have left our church to start new churches. It was probably a testimony of a departing team member that this man heard seven years earlier that left those words on his mind. In all, forty-two people moved from California to Tennessee to start the church there. Every church with a history has a cultural legacy.

2. *Shared experience.* Along with this accumulated legacy, churches have a recent history, the events within the last year and a half that a majority of the current congregation have shared. Recent events shape the culture. These experiences are collectively interpreted and sorted according to the basic mission of the church, and they are viewed in light of the solutions they offer. If a recent situation is labeled "a problem," then the church members intuitively identify which parts of the situation are "wrong"— out of step with where the church wants to go. The same is true when a situation that appears problematic is seen by the leaders as an opportunity.

The Coastlands now leases a former convent built in the early 1950s. When we got into the building, it needed extensive refurbishing, and I faced the dilemma of how to mobilize our people for the huge task. Though we would do all the restoration work ourselves, the materials would still cost approximately two hundred thousand dollars. One of our church values has always been a celebration of how God restores ravaged lives to their former beauty. We emphasize God as a restorer, and this tied in with the challenge before us. "We have an opportunity," I said, "to refurbish this building as a physical statement to our community that God delights in making new out of the old."

The people responded beyond my wildest expectations. As we worked on the building, we had ingrained in us even more deeply the mentality that God restores the old and worn. Every time we now walk into the building, we are reminded of that. Even if we had a chance to construct a new building, few in our church would want to.

When people go through things with one another—protracted illness, missions work, evangelistic crusades, the loss of a loved one, moving from one service to two on Sunday morning, and so on—they become bonded in their feelings. Even bad experiences, when shared, can produce happy memories. What happens to us shapes us. The same is true for churches.

3. *Folk society.* It may seem strange, even offensive, to speak of church as a tribal group, but it doesn't take long to recognize that every church is a subculture within itself. In church the elders stand around the fire (the coffee urn in the fellowship hall) telling stories about how it was in the good old days and passing down traditions of "how we've always done it." This tribal gathering usually happens in the fellowship lodge. Members also have favorite songs evoking sentimental thoughts. And each year on the pastor's anniversary, the church gives him a batch of freshly baked chocolate chip cookies, which everyone knows he loves. The folk culture is made up of the language, traditions, dress codes, patterns, and rites that are learned by church members as a result of being part of the group.

Every organization—even high-tech corporations—have "tribal customs" regarding symbols, language, rituals, and songs. Nevertheless, church culture is certainly different from unchurched culture. Believers and unbelievers have very different language, stories, codes, and symbols. And every individual congregation has its own unique cultural trappings that set it apart from other local churches. Your church logo (as a symbol) is unique, as is your stationery. One church may buy a new play structure for the children (a symbol of its interest in children's ministry); another church might put a world map in the foyer to mark its commitment to missions.

One element of the tribal society is the language appropriate in the organization. Some churches use "insider language" based on old hymns and the King James Bible. They would feel it unspiritual to talk any other way. At The Coastlands we made a conscious decision to use contemporary, imagistic language understandable to anyone walking in off the street. We avoid religious-sounding words and clichés because we want to reach a community of people who largely were not raised in church.

Churches also vary in how they conduct rituals such as baby dedications, baptisms, and Communion. We call the Pacific Ocean, which is a two-minute walk from our building, our baptismal. When we baptize several people during the summer months, we usually have a barbecue beforehand. In the winter we use hot tubs, which seems strange to most other churches but normal to our people. For us, baptism is an outdoor event. New believers in our church, who haven't known any other approach to baptism, would find it odd to observe the ritual taking place in a baptismal tank in the front of a church. Their question would probably be, "Don't these people have hot tubs?"

Folk societies also have rites of passage. The members of a church intuitively know the route a person normally must take to get into leadership, even though that's not codified. Woe to the pastor who tries to hurry a choice leadership prospect past the hoops. The outrage and opposition you may be facing to your choice of a new men's ministry leader might be because that new leader has not gone through the normal process imbedded in your church culture. Churches also have established, though unspoken, procedures for how children come into membership and are allowed to take Communion.

Additionally, every church has taboos. The person who tried to move that picture of Jesus out of the fellowship hall found out about taboos. Does anyone think the choir room really belongs to the whole church? Or what would happen to the usurper who tried to move Mrs. Magilicutty's class from the classroom she has used for twenty-five years? In church life something as simple as changing the location of the pulpit can cost a person his head. Service times and service lengths are also inviolable.

Then there's the dress code. Rarely is it in writing, but people soon learn whether to dress up or down at different weekly services. Wear the wrong thing, and you're branded as out of it or worldly or vain or disrespectful or rebellious. Wear the right thing, and you're modest or sharp or respectable. The first week when we started the Saturday night service, I opened my closet to dress for church and stood there in a daze. I didn't know what I was supposed to wear to Saturday night services. I'd never been to one, and so I had no cultural clue. I opted for a nice pair of Levis, and that has become the cultural norm.

4. *A network of relationships.* Each church has its own unique subculture of relational interconnections including groups that repel or attract others and opinion leaders with followers. These

networks are developed over long periods of time, and they have settled into relatively permanent groupings. They may be due to numerous factors; for example, having children the same age, attending choir, joining the church, serving on a mission team, or being related outside of the church.

Sixty adults who saw their church through four rough months between pastors seven years ago found themselves needing to reach out and support one another to survive. Now that survival is not in question, they are not as desperate to reach out to newer people; they are content with their "old friends." People who come together out of necessity to face a crisis often want to stay together out of convenience when the crisis is over.

About four and a half years ago I realized that as "friendly" as our church was, most of the friendliness was limited to people who already felt comfortable with one another. I knew that unless I shifted the fellowship patterns, we would unintentionally be "closed" to assimilating newcomers.

My solution was to recruit dozens of cell-group leaders from the ranks of our long-term members. They were soon too busy taking care of their newly formed cell groups to have any time to infect other "old timers" with *koinonitus* (C. Peter Wagner's famous name for the *fellowship disease*).

To understand a church, a leader must understand the relationship groups in the church. Individuals don't act in a vacuum or make decisions in isolation. Often what is called fellowship is no more than sanctifying the kind of socializing that goes on at the Kiwanas Club. The relationship network can act as a barrier to what we want to accomplish or be a natural conduit for change. The pattern of relationships in a church is nowhere near as spiritual as we imagine.

5. *The prevailing philosophy.* Over time, the important decision-makers in a church establish a definite opinion about how to view life around them. This has been called a group paradigm—a way to make sense out of life's data. Ultimately, the prevailing philosophy of a church is its primary vehicle for interpreting things. It is conceptual and compelling.

Philology is the study of how people use words—what they mean by using the words they do. For instance, a philosopher knows there must be some fundamental difference between a *stool* and a *chair* because those words are attached to different concepts by people. The boundaries of concepts and language interest the philosopher: chairs have backs, stools do not; chairs can have arms, stools cannot.

Though there will be diversity, every church comes to a prevailing understanding about key concepts such as truth, mission, and approach to ministry. Each church has beliefs, values, and assumptions that have more clear-cut boundaries than most pastors or parishioners realize. Take the notion of authority, for instance. When does something cease to be *authority* (a chair) and become *control* (a stool)? Can authority be the basis for legitimate relationship? Is church authority institutional and structural, or informational and optional? What effects does control have in a person's life, as opposed to the effects generated by authority? Rarely are such questions spelled out, but answers to such intuitive questions produce a group philosophy. This collective mind-set is shared by the important decision-makers in the church, and it infiltrates the deepest level of the congregation's thinking.

At The Coastlands, for instance, we have a definite view about authority. We believe that authority is an insufficient basis for relationship; only love and truth can support relationship. Authority is used to promote others, not yourself, and the more authority you give away to others by empowering them, the more authority you end up having.

Not long ago I became aware, through a series of incidents relayed to me by various people, that some of our cell-group leaders were functioning under a different philosophy. They were lapsing into one of authority's great temptations: telling people "under them" to submit, no matter what. Instead of finding ways to come under and serve people, leaders were defining their relationship with people in terms of authority and submission.

Authority only comes through obeying God and serving people; its goal can only be to serve others' desire to obey God themselves. What some of the cell leaders misread was our whole thinking about authority. I have since done teaching and made some structural changes in an attempt to counteract the distorted elements that were creeping into our church culture.

We also have a prevailing philosophy about people. We believe almost everyone can be discipled and nurtured into a role of discipling and nurturing others. We do not focus on the specially gifted few—we let the giftings of everyone emerge over time. Many churches have a philosophy that presumes most believers cannot be raised to significant levels of maturity and leadership. Your church philosophy about this issue can be viewed in a simple question: What is the essential difference between deacons and elders? A scriptural answer to the question is not as clear-cut as a cultural answer. In many churches deacons are the less spiritual task doers, while the elders are viewed as spiritual leaders.

6. *Atmosphere.* Churches have a prevailing mood. If a happy-go-lucky backslapper walks into a reverent church on Sunday and walks down the aisle, loudly calling out, "Hey, great to see ya! Praise God! Isn't Jesus wonderful!" everyone will be thinking, *What's wrong with that person? This is church!* Conversely, if a person with a quiet, reverent demeanor comes into a church that's an upbeat, "Nice to see you, didn't we have fun at the picnic last week?" kind of place, and sits down with hands folded and eyes closed, everyone will wonder, *What's her problem?* Is either atmosphere right or wrong? No, it's part of culture.

ADJUSTING THE CULTURE

Just as homeowners remodel their houses as children grow and family needs change, a church, if it is to remain effective, must continually adjust the culture and on occasion shift it in a major way. Good leaders are always making minor adjustments in the culture with the big picture in mind. We can no more change the culture in a church with one sermon or program than we can add a room to a house by just knocking out a wall. Adjusting culture is large scale. Coaxing change, the subject of chapter 5, is smaller scale.

Any pastor who has tried to import a program successful in another church, say Evangelism Explosion, and seen it fail miserably has experienced firsthand the steamrollering power of church culture. The church where the program worked successfully had a culture as conducive as a greenhouse for tomato plants. The church where the program was transplanted had a different environment: different soil acidity, different temperature, different rainfall. Their values, beliefs, mission, and history were all different, in some ways, hostile. The pastor could promote the program, pray, and preach sermons to rally the troops, but it was doomed to failure.

Culture takes years to materialize, and it may take years to change. We can't just stand up and announce, "We need to change the environment around here. We're going to be a warm, loving church." That isn't how culture is picked up.

Much has been written in recent years about the role of paradigms in change. Paradigms are the grids we all use for making sense of our world. A paradigm can be large scale, like naturalism, for example, which assumes that matter is all there is and that science can explain all phenomena. Someone who believes in God has a different paradigm from an atheist. Paradigms can also be small scale, helping us to make sense of family or work. We have talked in this book about paradigms for understanding church and leadership, such as a river versus a lake and a process versus an event.

People sometimes resist a particular change because they hold to an adverse paradigm whether they are conscious of it or not. Such paradigms limit or suggest available options. A paradigm for many Christians is that church takes place on Sunday morning, Sunday night, and Wednesday night. Such a given precludes them from even considering holding a service at a time that might reach more people. I heard about a church that changed its Sunday morning service to Sunday afternoon at two o'clock. They wanted to reach musicians who do late-night gigs and can't get up in the morning to go to church. For some people, going to church in the afternoon instead of morning would be a sacrilege. It isn't a sacrilege; it's just a different time to have church.

To introduce a new idea, we must help people see the validity of a new paradigm. Often this means going to the Bible to sort out which of our paradigms are cultural and which biblical. We must show the inconsistencies of the old paradigm, that it doesn't adequately reflect reality or Scripture. Cognitive dissonance opens them to considering a new paradigm that better explains reality.

If we can show how the pieces that don't fit their paradigm do fit ours, they'll probably buy into ours—given plenty of time. People are problem solvers. They want solutions. And that is what a paradigm shift is all about.

Adjusting the culture means creating a conducive environment. Toward that end, I offer four suggestions.

Blaze the trail. People aren't stupid. They know pastor's schedule is important, so where I put my time shows my priorities and fleshes out what I expect of others. If I moved into a new church that had an event mentality instead of a process mentality, for example, one thing I would do to convert the church to a lifestyle mentality would be to involve myself in breakfasts with a group of men every other week for four months. Through these breakfasts I could touch twelve men in the church every four months. The more familiar they became with me outside the pulpit, the more they would see church as a lifestyle. What I would talk about at those breakfasts would be crucial. I wouldn't talk about church events but about things going on in our personal lives. I would lead the way in openness, because the leader sets the intimacy level. Doing what I am preaching is critical.

Retool structures. We have to send tangible signals. We showcase values by what we change. Again I'll use the example of a change from an event mentality. A church that holds three services a week would send a huge signal if it considered canceling Sunday night or Wednesday night services. (We certainly would discover very quickly who does view church as an event!)

The organizational structure of a church has a powerful effect on its mentality. Someone has said that we shape our buildings and then our buildings shape us. The same is true of our programs and organizational structure. When attitudes prevail that we can't seem to change any other way, shaking up the structure is one (dangerous if your authority is not well established) option.

Most structure in church is artificial—its only purpose is to support and enable the true work of the church. I keep reminding our leaders that our cell-group structure exists only to help our people do the very thing they are supposed to do—that is, care for and disciple others.

Too easily the structures ossify and become entrenched. They serve themselves and fight to maintain the status quo. This happened to our cell-group structure a couple of years ago. Our cell groups were initially divided into two groupings that we called companies after the blessing Isaac bestowed on Jacob: "May God Almighty bless you and make you fruitful and multiply you, that you may become a company [congregation] of peoples" (Gen. 28:3 NASB). They did okay for several years, but I began feeling that we needed to start a third company. My feeling was based on the fact that we were not reaching the new people in the church. The cell groups in the existing companies had grown slightly complacent, lulled by sameness. So I had one of our other pastors start up and oversee another company. I had been telling the other company pastors that they needed to find a way to reach those newcomers. They weren't able to, so we restructured.

We found that adding a third company was like adding a third friend to a pair of friends. Two people can get along well, but add a third, and it almost always ends up two against one. The change unsettled several leaders and the two pastors overseeing the existing groups because they worried about competition. But that was all right, because in the long run we achieved the higher purpose I had in mind. The point was not to compete but to stimulate one another to more love.

Add rather than subtract. In an established church, I wouldn't challenge what exists by tinkering with main elements such as services or governmental structure. Instead, I would develop additional services or ad hoc committees. One way to do this is with open invitation gatherings: "Many of us care about the future of our church," I would announce. "Therefore, every Saturday afternoon from four o'clock until six o'clock, all are invited to join together to pray, study Scripture, and talk about the church. We want to discover what God has in mind for our church in the future."

With an open invitation I would remove anyone's ability to criticize that meeting for happening. Before I would make that public announcement, I would go privately and individually to the handful of people I thought would oppose what I wanted to do. "I want to let you know ahead of time about a meeting I'm going to publicly invite everyone in church to attend. The meeting is for those who want to seek the Lord together and talk about the future direction of our church. I know you care about where we're going, and so I want you to have a chance to clear your calendar beforehand. I value your input. We don't agree on everything, but we do agree this church has a future." By talking personally to critics beforehand I would welcome them in, rather than push them away.

Select and tell the right stories. Storytelling is powerful, but not just any stories will do. Culture-adjusting stories—drawn from what happened during the week to us or someone in the congregation or one of their neighbors, or on something out of Christian or secular media—must be purposefully and selectively told.

If your church is learning to evangelize "New Age" type people, don't tell a lot of stories about other sorts of people who are being saved. Deliberately relate anecdotes about the target people. We need to have an eye out for such stories. A host of interesting things happens in our churches, and scores of interesting stories appear in the media that we could relate. But we want to tell the stories that reinforce adjustments we seek in the culture.

When I wanted to reinforce the confidence of our church members so they wouldn't be confounded by the heavy mysticism of the New Age movement, I told this episode: "Christianity is different from any religion I've ever explored," a woman once told me. "I've had every experience you can imagine—out-of-body experiences, every kind of occultic thing—but this isn't like anything I have heard or seen before. This is like God coming to me rather than me going to God. It's right in my heart."

Relate a few anecdotes like that, and everyone in the church, even the most staid believer who vaguely remembers the time in ancient history when he got saved, will get excited about winning New Agers.

ENCOURAGING RISK

Most local churches have adopted the prevailing culture of the larger body of Christ that makes meaningful change difficult to achieve. One of the strongest elements of that larger culture is the avoidance of risk. The moral conservatism so clearly spelled out in the Word of God has become confused with every other type of conservatism (political, financial, institutional, and so on). Churches and leaders become intimidated by the prevailing norms of that larger culture and by the looming, doubt-building question, "What if it doesn't work?" James M. Kouzes and Barry Z. Posner sum up the dilemma of leaders when it comes to taking risks: "Risk is inherent in every successful innovation. Whenever leaders experiment with innovative ways of doing things, they put themselves and others at risk.... One of the most glaring differences between the leader and the bureaucrat is the leader's inclination to encourage risk-taking, to step out into the unknown and not play it safe."[2]

One of the few times I have second-guessed myself was when we were about to pioneer The Coastlands. As an associate pastor of The Church on the Way, one of the most successful churches in America, I had a bright future right where I was. One December Sunday as I sat enjoying a Christmas service in that big church—the choir, the decorations, the music—I thought, *You must be crazy to leave all this to go start a new church.*

Then I felt impressed by a defining question to my heart: *Are you willing to leave this home to go make a home that others will one day be as sad to leave as you are today?* It took me only a moment to answer that question. *Yes*, I decided. And I have never looked back.

Serving Christ requires taking one risk after another. Whether it's the risk of losing a friend by sharing the gospel with him or her or having a Sunday school class shrink while we are the teacher, Jesus calls us to be people who regularly go where we have never gone before *for his sake*. Not surprisingly, that mentality doesn't always characterize leaders or churches. Risk is dangerous and potentially painful. But if we don't step out of the boat as Peter did on the Sea of Galilee, we accomplish little for Christ. Churches that regard "Play it safe" as the eleventh commandment, sooner or later, plateau and die.

What characterizes the mind-set of risk-takers? What are the wise versus foolish ways to go about taking a risk? Is it possible for leaders to make mistakes without creating doubts about their abilities?

THE MIND-SET OF RISK-TAKERS

A willingness to take risks begins with the pastor and is caught by others. Check yourself for the following attitudes.

Be focused on winning rather than on not losing. When a basketball team with a big lead chokes in the final minutes, the announcers often comment that the team played as though they were attempting to avoid a loss rather than hungrily pursuing a win. When our imagination centers on the bad that could happen if things go wrong rather than on the good that could happen if things go right, we are playing not to lose. Ironically, in sports and in ministry, playing not to lose usually leads to a loss.

Be careful but not conservative. Many churches are controlled financially by the idea of playing it safe. They won't spend a dollar on something that may fail. At The Coastlands we are financially careful but not conservative. So what if we make a mistake—as long as a program has the possibility of advancing the kingdom?

By financially "careful" I mean that we have a prescriptive budget that is set by our church council each quarter of the year. It is a prescriptive, not a descriptive budget, telling us what each department *can* spend, not what each department *did* spend. Each staff person works within the confines of his or her line-item allowances. Some months the staff members may slightly overspend, and other months they underspend. The total budget figure is watched very closely by our financial director. We spend to the budget, not according to what money does or does not come in the offering. To smooth out the inevitable fluctuation of income from month to month, we have a "buffer savings" equal to one-fourth of the budget. We draw from the buffer savings in months when the tithes and offerings are below budget, and we fill it back up when we have a monthly surplus. It is the first item to receive supplies money until it reaches the one-fourth mark. After the buffer is full, the staff and I are allowed to present the council with our wish list for one-half of any remaining supplies income. The other half is controlled by the council.

In finances, we try to distinguish between matters of *faithfulness* and those of *faith*. Good stewards are faithful; they don't overspend or take huge risks with others' money. Most of our financial decisions are made in faithfulness to what Jesus has allotted to us. But sometimes the council and I see that the Lord is saying something to us—that we should do something in faith. In those cases, the issue is not what money we have but what promise we have.

In Scripture no one gained a testimony by playing it safe. None of those in the Hebrews 11 hall of fame were conservative in their approach to life. They were radical. Whatever God told them to do, they did.

Eliminate "failure" from your vocabulary. Great leaders never use the word *failure;* they rarely even think about it as a possibility. They are high on the success-achievement scale and low on the failure-avoidance scale. They talk about glitches or false starts. "Never mind," they say; "we learned a lot from that one. At least we know one more way this isn't going to work."

If we have a process mentality rather than a production mentality, we can survive mistakes. We can overcome many failures as long as we use them to develop a better way to do something in the future. So we have to develop in people an attitude that it is okay if they try something and don't succeed.

Be optimistic about future possibilities. Watch what happens in a football game when a tight end drops a pass in the end zone. When he runs back to the huddle, his teammates don't start beating up on him. Usually they pat him on the helmet and say, "Next time." Besides the fact that he's a big guy, there is a reason for that. Unless it is the two-minute drill at the end of the game, his teammates know they have another chance. They figure if they don't score on this series of downs, they'll punt and score the next time they have the ball. They tried a long bomb, but it didn't work; they'll try it again later. They ran off tackle and lost two yards; they'll run a sweep next time. Most churches desperately need an attitude that sooner or later something is going to work for them if they keep at it.

Be comfortable with bloopers. People sometimes think that everything is resting on one venture, and if it fails, they're a failure and all is lost. They take mistakes too seriously. People at The Coastlands get a kick out of my mistakes.

In the first year that we began Saturday night services, the Fourth of July came on a Saturday. I wondered whether to cancel the service. Being a persistent sort of guy, I decided to go ahead with it. At best, we had seventeen people show up. On Sunday morning, with a grin on my face, I told the church, "I can't believe I did that." They laughed and laughed. They thought it was fabulous that their pastor had blundered and was willing to laugh at himself. None of them would have scheduled church to conflict with fireworks, but they enjoyed the fact that I was getting smarter all the time.

When handled properly, mistakes can bring an atmosphere of warmth and love in the church. The very humanness of errors can actually pull us closer together in a spirit of acceptance and forgiveness. So don't try to avoid mistakes. Use them for the sake of the kingdom.

Embrace failures as resources. Mistakes are not a total loss; on the contrary, they are an invaluable resource. We can always learn something if we have a mind-set of capitalizing on mistakes. Just as problems can be seen as opportunities, mistakes can be viewed as lessons.

Missteps are really just an inevitable part of the process. We are going somewhere; perhaps we will take a false step here; maybe our knees will buckle as we go there; but we're moving. Even if we have to crawl for a while, we learn things on our knees that we never learn by walking upright.

I try to remember that though I plan my path, the Lord directs my steps. Sometimes things just turn out differently than I planned. When a leader is completely willing to acknowledge bad choices, sinful attitudes, and other points of personal culpability, mistakes do not threaten that leader's credibility.

Chapter Eight

POSITIONING RESOURCES

Some four hundred teaching tapes I had accumulated through the years from churches and seminars were hogging space in my library, so one day I decided to put them to better use. I thought about giving them to staff members, pastor friends, cell-group leaders, or the entire church. Finally I settled on the masses. I piled the tapes in big baskets, and for two weeks I had them passed out to people in the church foyer on their way into church. Later, during the service, I talked about further distribution: A person might have a tape number three from a series and would need to ask around for the rest of the seminar. I wanted everyone to pass the tapes on after listening. The "tape club" turned out to be a big hit. People thanked me for giving them valuable listening for their commutes, and I was excited, because in one stroke, four hundred teaching sessions were introduced into the life of our church.

This is a small-scale example of strategic positioning. We need to use our resources—people, time, money, spiritual gifts, and sermons, among many other things—in a way that most effectively accomplishes our mission. That doesn't happen spontaneously. Strategic positioning is a broad way of talking about planning. Even something as small as getting the most benefit from these audiotapes required planning. First, I had to choose which tapes to give and which to keep. Then, before I could think about a method of distribution, I had to decide who would get them. Finally, I had to figure the logistics of how to encourage maximum distribution among people in the church. On a much larger scale, the same should happen with all our resources.

I have saved this subject until now for a good reason. Most leaders want to race ahead to the business of planning programs and events before they have done the proper groundwork. Strategic positioning is much more than arranging logistics. We shouldn't plan an event without knowing how it relates to the overall mission of the church and without understanding such things as the resources and distinctives of our church and the needs of our world.

IS PLANNING BIBLICAL?

Many Christians, misinterpreting Jesus' words "Do not worry about tomorrow, for tomorrow will worry about itself" (Matt. 6:34), are ambivalent about even the idea of planning. But the Bible has more to say on the subject. Paul speaks specifically about planning in 2 Corinthians 1:15–17, and in other epistles he recounts travel plans and organizes the activities of his ministry team. Isaiah 32:8 says, "The noble man makes noble plans, and by noble deeds he stands."

It is no more spiritual to be unplanned than planned. Certainly one can plan in a natural way, presumptuously and with an attitude of self-direction. But godly strategic positioning is not coming up with our own plans and then asking God to bless them. It is not human ingenuity sanctified by a quick closing prayer. Godly planning is responsible obedience. It is understanding what God is saying to our church and then posturing ourselves to fulfill his purposes. Planning is good stewardship.

In the early years after planting The Coastlands, we set aside money in a sanctuary account to buy land and someday construct a building. Several years ago I felt impressed of the Lord that we should give away everything in the sanctuary account to provide a sanctuary for the homeless. I felt an assurance from the Lord that if we built a sanctuary for the poor, the time would come when God would build a sanctuary for us.

So instead of forming our own ministry to the homeless, we investigated every outreach to the homeless in our county, secular or Christian. We decided the best was a shelter sponsored by a church from another denomination about ten miles away. We donated our money to buy building supplies so they could enlarge their facility, and we organized our people to help in several work parties. Since that other church has an incredible outreach to the homeless, when homeless people come our way, we happily refer them to this center. Why duplicate a ministry that is already effective?

As this illustrates, the best use of thousands of dollars and thousands of people hours are at stake in the direction a church takes. More often than not, those who oppose planning end up being poor stewards. Strategic positioning means deciding prayerfully where our resources should best be spent and planning accordingly.

Often the issue is not waste but diversion. Without strategic positioning we can easily get sidetracked by worthy causes from the unique work God has for our congregation. For example, a host of special-interest groups and parachurch ministries want to use the people of our congregations to accomplish their missions. I'm not against such ministries. I applaud their work, and many at The Coastlands are involved with them. But I do resist the notion that all Christians and churches ought to be involved in certain causes. Just because the church down the street has a ministry to the homeless doesn't mean that your church ought to.

Finally, planning is not only biblical, it is the wise course of action. You don't have to pastor a medium-to-large-size church for long to know that without planning, you have mayhem. If a single man wanted to travel across the United States and he had plenty of time and money on his hands, he probably could do fine without an itinerary. Wander from town to town, get a hotel here or there—that makes for adventure. But if this man was married, had two small children and a limited amount of time and money, and tried the same unplanned adventure, he would have a carful of unhappy campers.

The same principle holds true in church. It is one thing for an individual leader to have a sense of what God wants him or her to do day by day and then carry it out; it is an altogether different thing to get a group of people to cooperate and move in the same direction.

Strategic positioning involves seven elements. Working through all seven steps can be a major undertaking the first time through, but each step is essential. And once you have laid the foundation, many steps in the process become intuitive and far simpler. The first step in strategic positioning is a return to your purpose.

MIND YOUR MISSION

When leaders don't know what to do next, it is often because they don't know what they are supposed to be doing ultimately. They don't know the next step because they haven't chosen a direction to walk. The basis for strategic positioning is a clear understanding of the mission of the church. The moment we lose sight of the mission, we begin to stray and waste resources. Therefore, strategic positioning is not a reaction to the past, an effort to play catch-up with what has already happened; rather, it looks to mold the future.

The key to doing the right things is knowing the mission and investing all church resources into that mission. Knowing your mission dramatically impacts your scheduling. For example, I thought about our mission at The Coastlands and made a list of all the "one anothers" in the New Testament: love one another, be kind to one another, and so on. I then divided them into two lists, the first being the one anothers best accomplished in a formal meeting, and the second being those best accomplished in informal settings. To my distress, I found that there aren't many one anothers best suited for a structured meeting.

Now wait a second, I said to myself. *My job is to teach people how to live their Christian lives—how to do these one anothers to one another—but I'm using a setting that prevents one anothers from happening!*

I tried to console myself with the notion that our formal meetings gave people the understanding and fuel they needed to do the one anothers. The problem is, if a premium is put on everybody gathering together to listen to the pastor, and little organized direction is given to what people do outside the structured setting, pretty soon, people catch on. They realize what is most important to the pastor. Spiritual maturity is regarded ipso facto as showing up at church and listening to sermons. But with a clear sense of our mission, I knew I had to plan into our church schedule how our people would get the one anothers done. What we settled on was to have only one primary worship service a week with the rest of the emphasis being on cell groups.

Make sure you define your mission in terms of tangible results. When one young couple first came to our church three years ago, they had nearly suffered the trauma of divorce. All kinds of wrongs had destroyed their relationship. As I counseled with them, I gave them this image: "You are like a forest that has suffered a fire. All the trees have been singed and burned, and the grass is gone. But I'm looking forward to the day when green grass begins to sprout again, when the trees begin to bud and blossom, and you are once again refreshed by gentle rains." It took time, but today this couple is full of the life of Jesus. Their marriage is a verdant, lush forest. Restoration such as that is how I measure effectiveness in our church. That is the fulfillment of our mission: People loved this couple; they have been mended; and now they are being trained to minister to other couples.

Here is a helpful exercise to translate your mission into tangible resource positioning. Imagine that in tomorrow's mail you receive an envelope addressed to you with no return address. When you open up the envelope, out falls a check for thirty thousand dollars made out to your church. The enclosed letter reads: "Dear Pastor, I've been watching you for some time, and I've determined that what you want to accomplish for the Lord is worth investing in. This is the first of as many installments as you need. In the future, if you need another check for thirty thousand dollars, simply tug on your right ear twice during your sermon and another check for thirty thousand dollars will be on your desk the following week." How would you spend that thirty thousand dollars? What kind of program or staff would you arrange?

Oh, one other thing. There is a postscript at the bottom of the letter that could make the exercise more difficult: "P.S. You may not use any of this money for land or buildings." Now, how would you spend that unlimited supply of money? If you have a hard time answering that question, that may explain why you don't have all the money you have been praying for!

The exercise still isn't over. Often we presume that bigger is better. "If we just had more staff." But that isn't always true. Deep-pocket sponsors have tried in the past to build churches by throwing money at them but have found that growth isn't automatic. So after you devise your plan for how to spend all this money, you must explain to this donor how your spending plan will accomplish your church's mission. Can you justify an investment of thirty thousand dollars into your church process?

MAINTAIN IDENTITY

A central issue in strategic positioning is organizational integrity. It is a given that individuals in the organization must have integrity, being true to the Word of God and living by the same standards in private as they do in public. Another crucial aspect of personal integrity, though, is to be true to what God made us to be. An impostor may live a moral life, but he or she still lacks integrity. If I am not true to God's workmanship in my life—scrambling about trying to be like other people or putting on a false front—then I am not a person of integrity. Likewise, an organization must have integrity both about doing what is right and about being what God wants it to be.

Therefore, the second step in strategic positioning is to ask, "Who are we?" A congregation must stick with its distinctives. We don't want to plan programs and activities that clash with who we are. Too often when churches plan for the future, they want to imitate a popular program in another church. They try to abandon their congregational personality to implement the program, but it rarely works.

Our congregation is all about recovering people and mobilizing them in ministry. You could look at our program and fault us for not sponsoring outreach events like street witnessing. But we see many people come to know Jesus even without such an outreach focus. We believe that if we mend and mobilize people, they become winsome to neighbors and friends. We do evangelism in a way that fits who we are.

Another of our values is servanthood. Therefore, when we plan an event, we want to maximize the number of people involved to pull it off. We don't want to schedule an event that requires just one or two workers, and we certainly don't want to conduct an event that must be led by the same person who led it last year.

At one leadership retreat I asked our leaders to identify distinctives of our church. The exercise turned out to be pleasurable and enlightening to all, accompanied by laughter and by light-bulbs going on all over the room. Here is what they came up with:

Our Orientation	The Opposite Orientation
Innovative	Traditional
Focused on the future	Focused on the present and the past
Releasing people	Keeping people
Exporting	Importing
Network of colleagues	Hierarchy of subordinates
Serving	Being Served
Action	Deliberation
Risk-taking	Playing it safe
Effectiveness of the church	Size of the church

Consider doing this exercise with your leaders. As you think about your distinctives, pay attention to the following elements: values, attitudes, atmosphere and feeling of your gatherings, perspectives on issues, and criteria for decision making and problem solving.

ASSESS WHERE YOU STAND

Before positioning your resources for fulfilling your mission, you obviously must know what your resources are. You probably have much more going for you than you realize. Inventory and assess the following areas.

Strengths and weaknesses. Some of the strengths of The Coastlands are

1. A high level of involvement in and awareness of the lives of fellow congregants. We are open with one another and rarely feel as if our problems are that unusual.

2. We have well-developed sense of purpose and values, and we are not afraid to try new things.

3. We are structured in our staff and ministry groups to function well without daily involvement with me as the leader. This allows me the opportunity to travel extensively.

Some of the weaknesses of The Coastlands are

1. We are poor at organized evangelism, such as canvassing a neighborhood. I don't know if I could get my people to do such a thing.

2. We are decentralized, scattered, with each cell group doing its own thing. With our weekend worship service as our only common ground, it is nearly impossible to try to collect the whole church together at another time for an event. I am concerned about that and am working on it right now. We have a unified vision, but we are not as cohesive a group as we once were.

3. Our people attend church when they want, and that's it. The notion that they should come because they are good Christians is nonexistent.

Key personnel. Who are your leaders, staff, volunteers, opinion shapers, and potential workers? Getting each one in the right spot is one of your main jobs. A soccer coach finds some kids are better as goalies because they are aggressive and smart. Other kids are fast on their feet, so the coach makes them midfielders or rovers. Some kids have a powerful kick but are clumsy, so the coach puts them in back as defenders. When a person in church can't seem to get in sync, their position may be the problem.

A certain woman in our church can generate more work in five minutes than most human beings can generate in five weeks. She used to supervise our graphics department until one day I said to her, "I'm going to move you out of graphics. I want you to take over children's ministries."

"There is so much still to be done," she objected.

"Let me put it to you this way," I said. "If you don't move out of this graphics department, not only will you reinvent every form known to humankind, you'll give us seven variations on each form. I want to put you someplace where we can use all your energy."

She was tortured by the change, but when she took over children's ministries, it went into hyperspeed in every direction. She transformed the department, and now visitors marvel at a church program for kids that has assemblies interesting anough to attract even adults and has hallways decorated with fishing nets, pier pilings, large treasure chests, and all sorts of other nautical accessories. People at different times doing different things is what leadership is all about.

Programs and activities. Programs include ongoing and seasonal ministries such as Sunday school, vacation Bible school, counseling centers, and Promise Keepers.

Physical plant. How much of your building is used each week? What off-campus facilities do you or can you use? How user-friendly are your buildings? What restrictions do you need to overcome?

Realistic budget. Develop a budget that is prescriptive rather than descriptive—that is, decide how the money should be spent to fulfill the mission rather than merely continuing present spending.

Intangibles. What is the morale, mood, and spiritual atmosphere of the church?

In the previous section I described the exercise our leaders went through to identify our distinctives. At that same meeting we also answered a series of questions to better understand ourselves, our resources, and our future needs. We found that not only did we learn a lot, but it built our morale. Here are those questions:

- What five words best describe our church?
- To what sort of people is our church most attractive? Least attractive?
- For the types of people who think our church is attractive, list any needs they may have (for example, parent training courses, financial counseling, and so on).
- What reasons would you give to a friend as to why he or she should come to our church?
- List everything about our church that you really like— especially the strengths or things that make us different from other churches you have attended.

The question about whom your church benefits is a crucial one. Certain people like your church for a reason, and that reason is a resource to keep in mind throughout the process of strategic positioning. Our leaders decided that we are least attractive to stereotypical Harley riders with leathers and long hair, the elderly (mostly because our music is on the loud side), and people with a lot of religious training. We are most attractive to families with small children (because we put so much emphasis on our children's ministry) and to honest people seeking answers to life's questions.

UNDERSTAND THE TIMES

We can't plan in a cocoon. Since we are called to reach our society, the state of our society directly affects our strategic positioning. What are the needs of the people we intend to win? For clues I look to many sources.

I stay alert to trends because they can give me prophetic insight into what I should do as a pastor and into what we should do as a church. Recently, I asked myself, *Why are fast-food chains offering wider variety in their menus?* Many people would say that it is because of the ethnic mix in our culture. We have people from so many different national origins that the franchises want to sell food that suits their taste.

That is a nice thought, but that isn't the primary reason that fast-food restaurants are offering more variety. You know why they have the variety if you have more than two children and have ever made the fateful mistake of saying, "Hey, kids, let's go out for dinner tonight. Where do you want to go?" One child wants to go to one fast-food place, and another kid wants to go to some other restaurant. Fast-food chains are balancing the franchise mentality (do one thing and do it cheaper and better than the competition) with the demands of the new consumer. People want and expect options.

This consumer demand for variety has implications for the church. Perhaps we ought to begin offering more options in ministry. In a midweek service, instead of the pastor giving one sermon, several classes could be offered. The people could gather for worship and then break up for classes.

Another way to figure out the culture is to consider the latest how-to books, for they give us an indication of the issues about which people are concerned. What traumas are people trying to get over? What advice is the secular world dishing out? What terminology of the world can we adopt? My former pastor once said that there is a huge difference between relating to the world *in* its terms and relating to the world *on* its terms. We can't do the latter, for we proclaim God's will without compromise, but we can convey God's will in the language of the people.

To most people, religious words are blank words. Even most religious people, for example, don't know what *sanctification* means. Like missionaries we must translate kingdom ideas into the language of our culture. Instead of using the word *sanctification,* I might say, "We are always in process, always a people in recovery, spiritually, emotionally, relationally, morally." My hope is that somebody who doesn't know anything about God or the Bible can hear that and say, "I get it."

CONSIDER THE POSSIBILITIES

At this stage we want to generate ideas by identifying crucial issues to address. As we consider the first four elements—our mission, distinctives, church environment, and cultural environment—many opportunities and possibilities for action will suggest themselves (see figure 8.1). We won't be able to address them all—the next step involves prioritizing—but for now we want to creatively consider the strategic possibilities.

Sometimes a single element suggests the issues we must address. For example, if a church decides that its purpose is to be a missionary-minded church, among other things, the church may want to hold two missions conventions a year.

Other times the interplay between elements points to crucial issues. For example, if our purpose includes evangelism, yet we noted that our church is weak in the area of evangelism, that calls our attention to one of our strategic issues. Or if one of our strengths is showing mercy, and we have noticed an increasing problem of homelessness in our community, we see a strategic opportunity.

Figure 8.1

The Process of
STRATEGIC POSITIONING

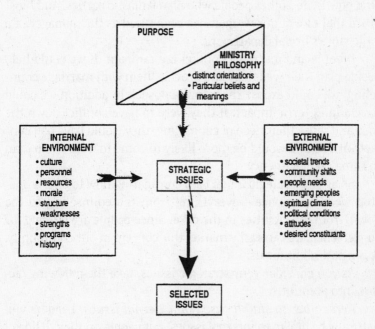

PURPOSE

MINISTRY PHILOSOPHY
• distinct orientations
• Particular beliefs and meanings

INTERNAL ENVIRONMENT
• culture
• personnel
• resources
• morale
• structure
• weaknesses
• strengths
• programs
• history

STRATEGIC ISSUES

EXTERNAL ENVIRONMENT
• societal trends
• community shifts
• people needs
• emerging peoples
• spiritual climate
• political conditions
• attitudes
• desired constituents

SELECTED ISSUES

ARRANGED PROCESS

EVALUATION

Recently, I have had some creative ministry ideas as a result of the strategic positioning process. One priority at The Coastlands is community exposure—convincing people that church is for them, not against them. As I assess our resources, I note that our building offers a gorgeous setting for indoor or outdoor weddings. We also have excellent seamstresses in our church, who sew wedding gowns, and other people who plan fantastic parties. And I just heard that one of our women has been hired as the manager of a large store's bridal department.

Divorce and marriage conflict are rampant. If we could help people plan their weddings and provide them with marriage counseling, we could expose them to the gospel. In addition we could have a long-term impact. If they were to have conflict down the road and sense their need of counseling, they would have had contact with us and would be more likely to come to us for help than to some secular agency.

So as one strategic issue, I am considering how to offer a one-stop wedding service—everything from the counseling to the gown, from the facilities to the cake. Since people are looking for convenience, we can easily market this concept in our community. It is a natural fit for us.

As you consider your strategic issues, take the following factors into account.

Remember to stay focused on external issues. Leaders will naturally be drawn to internal issues, but people on the outside of your church have no champion to speak for them. Most of our internal problems have no relation to the outside world. We can run from one internal problem to another trying to keep insiders happy and comfortable, but we will never get to the crying needs of our world. Over time, an ingrown church dies.

We must link our church's survival to our responsiveness to key external issues. The unspoken assumption most people have goes like this: *If we stay the same, we have a greater chance of surviving or succeeding than if we risk doing something new.* Actually the opposite is true. Unless we respond to what is going on around us, our congregation will dwindle and die. We have to focus on the people who are thinking or should be thinking about coming to our churches.

Stay connected to your history. Enterprises that have no relationship with our past usually fail. For example, if you try to move from a traditional, liturgical church service to seeker services in one dramatic move, you will almost certainly fall flat on your face. You will need to take small steps in that direction in order to build up some history.

TAKE AIM

It is impossible to address every need. Out of many options, at this stage we identify the strategic issues. What two or three issues should the church tackle now? We should make our decisions with the following factors in mind.

Build on strengths and successes. Completely new ventures are rarely productive. Your church has already developed competency in certain things. In the future you want to capitalize on those abilities. The most important thing to build on is the pastor's gift mix. If the pastor lacks experience in an area, for instance, drama, you don't want to launch a drama ministry that is expected to present a skit every Sunday morning.

Smaller churches often overlook their strengths and resources. Church size does affect what we can or cannot do, but that doesn't mean small churches can't do much. What they must do is find ministries suited for their special abilities. A church may be comprised of a small group of elderly people. It isn't growing much, but people aren't leaving, either. The stability of this church is their great asset. Such a congregation is ideally suited to helping missionaries, providing care packages and remembering the missionary kids' birthdays.

Focus your energies. In a house that is messy from basement to attic, you make a greater impact by cleaning one room spotlessly than by picking up one or two things in each room. Realistically, even the most missions-minded of churches cannot go into *all* the world. Rather than scattering its energies, a church can have a bigger impact if it selects one nation or area into which it will pour its resources. The Coastlands has focused its energies in

Western Europe, primarily in Norway and Switzerland, first establishing beachheads with one congregation through various ministry exchanges and then following up other opportunities. For us, the only legitimate use of short-term missions is going back to the same place over and over until real relationships are formed.

Look for bridges to needs. For instance, retired school teachers in your church can be the bridge to the children of your community. They can go to the local junior high school principal and offer their services at an after-school tutorial program for children based at your church facility. This service would be a blessing to the school and to working parents who don't have the time to do what your church offers to do for them. Such serving builds institutional credibility with the community.

POSITION RESOURCES

Strategic positioning ultimately comes down to arranging the resources and elements of your church to support your objectives and to address strategic issues. Does your budget reflect your priorities or the spending habits of the past? Are your people in positions where they are effective and growing, or have they stagnated? As you position resources, keep the following things in mind.

Introduce new elements into the environment and remove obsolete ones. Christians are great at birthing programs and lousy at intentionally killing them. But both are necessary. Killing programs is often the only way to free the resources necessary to move in strategic, new directions.

No one has enough money or time to do everything. My administrator loves to tell me, "If we spend money on this project, it means we won't have money to spend on that other project." Coming face-to-face with that reality always bothers me. But I have learned that unless our resources increase, I can't add to our program before we let something else go. Right now I'm having to let some of our staff go so that we have the money to acquire newer technology for more ministry.

Reposition current elements. Adjusting current resources can often solve what seems like an intractable problem. Four areas of church life will particularly require regular tinkering.

1. *Your theme*. What are you teaching? We went through a season in which God spoke to us about his sovereignty—that he is the God who calls the dawn and numbers the days until a mountain goat gives birth (Job 38:12; 39:1). Despite sometimes tragic and disappointing circumstances, he is still in charge and in control. But that season did not last forever. The teaching theme now is different than it was then. We are studying how differently God see things from the way people do. At other times we have looked at the implications of new wineskins, recovery, and the like.

2. *Activities*. Because we are trying at The Coastlands to help people who don't know God well to know him better, I decided to have a treasure hunt. I invited people to come to church from noon until 1:30 P.M. on Tuesdays with their lunch and their Bible. I said I would answer any questions on any subject. About forty-five people came and enjoyed it thoroughly. It gave them the feeling that studying the Bible isn't so intimidating, that it can be fun. Though the treasure hunt was successful, we discontinued it after a few months. It had served a purpose, but it was then time to shift the resources of my time elsewhere.

3. *Training*. When people in the church are going to do new things, we need to empower them with knowledge and skills. Ask yourself, *What do we need to change about how we are mobilizing and developing people to accomplish our goals?*

4. *Structure of staff and volunteers*. Just as we wouldn't want to wear the same wardrobe in summer and winter, we often will find that the church should not wear the same structure at all times. A new season requires a new wardrobe. That doesn't mean we must permanently get rid of anything; we may want to put it in the closet and bring it back later.

Balance long-range objectives with short-range agony. Someone has said that leadership is mostly about long-range planning followed by short-range suffering for the sake of that long-range plan. To accomplish something over time, we generally must sacrifice in the immediate future. Helping people through that pain is part of our job.

Assign responsibilities. Make people accountable for new things. If you have a choice between giving a job to an old guard member or new guard, give preference to the new. Design the process to address the strategic issues and accomplish the mission, not to accommodate long-time Christians.

I recently reconsidered how we could better position the resources of our church to accomplish our mission of helping people recover. Figure 8.2 shows my process of thinking.

First, I had to take into account the causes of the problem. If I wanted to plan how to fix people, I had to understand how people become torn. Second, I needed to plan various means that would likely help people recover from what had torn them. Third, I needed to work at prevention and further strengthening of those who are healthy. Finally, I asked, "How can we introduce two or three of these healthful elements in the next several months?" The whole exercise took about forty-five minutes.

There is one final element to strategic positioning, and it is one that most people leave off: evaluation. If we don't know our strengths and weaknesses, we will do an inadequate job of planning for the future. The vital step of evaluation is covered in detail in chapter 9.

Strategic positioning is a way for an entire organization to get in agreement with the Lord, to say yes to him with our church structures, systems, and programs. Individually we are admonished to love and serve God with the vital parts of our life—our heart, our soul, our mind, and our strength. Strategic positioning helps a church process do the same thing with its vital parts.

Figure 8.2

MENDING PEOPLE:
An Example of Strategic Positioning

1. How do people become torn in their soul?

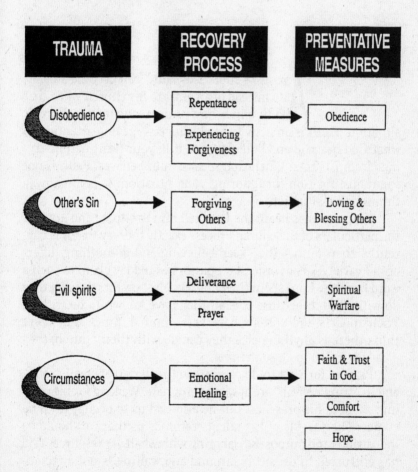

Chapter Nine

EVALUATING RESULTS

A pastor's supposed "faith" can become a liability instead of an asset to his church when that faith blinds him to the reality of his church's situation. Faith is an activity of obedience—paying attention to what God has said and holding on to it in your heart despite trying circumstances. When God speaks, faith believes. Faith is not vague justification for ignoring your situation. It is a pathway through that situation.

If a pastor has heard the Lord tell him to situate and arrange the particulars of the church process exactly the way that it is currently, then faith—the "keep-believing-and-do-nothing-differently" variety—is in order. Few pastors would lay claim to such a word from the Lord about their church. Most pastors do what they do with church because it is all they have known to do with it. Their models and options have been limited. Since they don't think there is anything else they can do with their church, they plead with God to do something.

Prayers for God to do "something really great, really soon" and to "bring revival," are always appropriate. We long for his coming; we need his presence. But he also told us to occupy until he comes. The parable of the talents reminds us that we should be industrious and purposeful, laboring with whatever resources God has entrusted to us; sitting around and waiting is not a recommended course of action. Yet many church leaders fix their eyes on the sky, resigned in their minds that God's work can only be addressed spiritually. They pray for more leaders instead of making disciples; they ask God to stir up the people instead of mobilizing and inspiring those people themselves.

Sometimes the answers to what ails church or to what might enhance its impact are a bit more organic than our faith wants to believe. Several weeks ago a pastor came to see me in the hope that I might be able to counsel him in his discouraging church situation. His congregation was even smaller now than the sixty people he had inherited from the previous pastor three years earlier. People would visit but not stick around. The pastor hadn't been able to develop any leaders, so he and his wife did most of the work. Now the worship leaders were leaving the church too.

I asked this gentle, good man a few questions. I discovered that he lived forty minutes away from the community in which he pastored; he never met any of the men in informal, ongoing meetings, such as at breakfast; he had no personal burden for the community; and the town was right in the middle of a huge economic change—the largest employer had just shut down and moved away.

Of course, he had been praying. God sometimes puts the handwriting on the wall, however, and it was time for the pastor to take an honest look at his church situation. His problems were obvious, not spiritual. Without changing his living situation and investing himself more in the few people he did have in the church, he might as well resign now.

Another pastor friend of mine has served as an overseer of several churches. I don't think the role suits him or his giftings well; the number and the quality of the churches for which he is responsible have gone down. His personal finances have too. But when I pressed my friend to evaluate his tenure—either to conclude something about his personal suitability for the role or about his strategies and arrangements—he kept defending things. An honest look at results would tell him that he did not have the gift mix for the job or that he needed a new battle plan. His fear of being evaluated as a failure kept him in a posture (status quo) in which he could not possibly succeed—unless God miraculously intervened.

Both pastors put their hope in a supernatural solution to their situations when opportunities and options for natural developments existed. They were not as stuck as their desperate prayers indicated. Neither pastor was willing to change; each wanted God to change everything for him.

One of the most important processes in church leadership—evaluation—is the easiest to neglect, but we overlook it to our loss. If we don't know what we have done right, we can't build on it as effectively for the future. If we don't know why something failed, we will likely repeat our mistakes. Effective leaders regularly evaluate their organizations because they know organizations produce the results they are designed to produce. Poor results usually come from faulty design. Evaluation forces us to face the results of our work and ask the hard questions about how our processes, plans, and strategies are contributing to such outcomes.

Some church leaders are like golfers who refuse to take lessons. They hit the ball all over the course. Each time it ends up in an unlikely spot or strays too far to the right, they act surprised and upset: "I can't believe it. What's wrong with that stupid ball?" The truth of the matter is that there is no real surprise; the ball always goes exactly where it is driven by the mechanics of their swing.

SAY AAAHHHH

Like a sick person avoiding a doctor's checkup, church leaders tend to shun evaluation. Evaluation can be uncomfortable, especially if we haven't done it before. No matter what our church size, we dread hearing criticism and facing up to mistakes as much as an overweight person hates hearing about the need to change eating habits. If we have been sincere in most of our efforts at church, it can be disheartening to learn that sincerity did not carry the day.

Another reason we may avoid evaluation is the pressure of keeping up with today and tomorrow. Evaluation doesn't have as much urgency to it as writing our Sunday sermon or dealing with the Sunday school staffing problem.

As I have already explained, another reason church leaders avoid evaluation is theological. If things aren't going well, we rationalize, "It's God's will," or "All that matters is that we're faithful." Clearly faithfulness is vital, but it can be an excuse for sustaining the status quo. We sense the job is not getting done, we don't know why, and we content ourselves with faithfulness; that is, fruitless, hard work. God wants us to be both faithful and effective. These are not mutually exclusive concepts.

Effectiveness is not synonymous with size. Is a big church a good church? Is a small church a failure? No one is comfortable with those notions. Leaders of churches that have had numerical success can humbly say, "It's just the Lord." I appreciate their attitude of not wanting to take glory for themselves, but have we thought through the implications of that statement? Does that mean God wants to bless some churches but not others? Is it "just the Lord" when a church doesn't do well? Although everyone will claim not to equate church size with church success (quality), our traditional church paradigm offers us no other ways to evaluate how good a job a church is doing. But at best, numbers tell us only part of the story. For instance, a church planted in a booming suburb of a fast-growing city may well attract huge numbers of people, not because of anything especially noteworthy done by the pastor, but because it is the only show in town.

Large-church pastors are as intimidated by evaluation as are small-church pastors. We fear being told we aren't doing a good job. We dread the final pronouncement, "Poorly done, thou bad and faithless servant." On the other hand, we are eager to make our lives count for more; and we can't define *more* without taking an honest look at the job we are presently doing. Those of us who want to do a better job at pastoring—no matter what the costs— ask for evaluation. We want help in knowing what we might do differently. As long as we can see evaluation as a tool to achieve excellence, we can endure the pain of it.

The problem is, how do we assess the relative quality of a church process? How do we put a yardstick on love? Trying to evaluate the quality of a church is much like attempting to determine how good a college is. In the field of higher education, researchers have been trying for decades to arrive at a meaningful model with which to evaluate the quality of education students receive at various colleges. The folklore of college quality tends to focus on three factors: (1) quality of graduates—achievement test results, salaries after graduation; (2) quantity of resources—number of library books, faculty Ph.D.s; (3) institutional visibility—size, name recognition, tradition. Researchers know, however, that these are not legitimate indications of quality because, for example: (1) the reason such bright people graduate from Harvard is because such bright people enter as freshmen—the output is determined primarily by the input; (2) there is no correlation between institutional assets and students' intellectual development; and (3) colleges become well-known through their sports programs, their highly visible professors, and their bigness—none of which actually impacts upon the average student.

In other words, measurements of quality that are easily translated into numbers rarely tell the story of college quality. The same is true for churches. Quality ought to be a statement of what actually happens to people who attend a college or a church. Are they affected by their church/college experience? What changes occurred in them that would not have occurred had they not attended that church?

Leadership skill makes a difference. A church does not have to grow in size to be considered effective, but the people ought to sense that they are fulfilling the mission God has given them, whether that is shaping the lives of the seven people in a rural community who have been in the church for forty years, or dealing with the seven hundred who have recently come to the church because of a new housing development.

Leaders in situations where the kingdom doesn't seem to be gaining ground often live with the painful fear that they are out of God's will or outside of God's blessing. But before someone makes God the fall guy for why a church hasn't been effective, we should try evaluating and tinkering with the systems and the processes of that church.

MAKING MINISTRY MEASURABLE

If effectiveness is not about size or wealth, if merely counting the attendance or weekly offerings doesn't tell much, what does?

Effectiveness is the measure of how much of what a church intends to accomplish (its mission) it actually does accomplish. So the first step in evaluation is to define effectiveness in measurable terms related to the institutional mission and the constituents of the church. We can define effectiveness in terms of (1) numbers or (2) ideal processes.

1. Are you reaching numeric goals for things like Sunday attendance, conversions, baptisms, income, missions giving, people who complete a leadership training group, and cell groups?

At The Coastlands I am interested in the number of churches we have planted. We have started fourteen in the last eleven years, which may sound like a lot, but I don't think so, because we are behind schedule. Because our mandate from heaven is to plant churches, we ought to have planted more.

Another number I watch closely is the number of cell groups with apprentice leaders. That tells me what we will be able to do in the future. Until I made some recent changes in our cell-group structure, we had slipped to having sixteen of our sixty-one cell groups without apprentices. Evaluation told me we needed to change things. Now we have forty-five groups, and only three are without apprentices.

Numbers aren't everything, but they can tell you much about the health and future possibilities of the church.

2. Assess how close the existing church process or program is to the ideal. As we pray and think about our churches, we ought to be able to envision an ideal process or environment, such as the existence of certain programs or systems for counseling, evangelism, teaching, follow-up, accountability, and leadership training. I evaluate the quality of our institution not just in terms of numeric results but also in terms of how close we are getting to my ideal vision for various components of the whole church process. The closer we are getting to the ideal, the more effective we should be.

As I mentioned in chapter 3, early in the life of our church, I knew I wanted a counseling program that was run by laypeople who mentor other laypeople. I envisioned counseling that was based on Scripture and revelation rather than clinical psychotherapy. When that program came into existence, I took that as a measure of effectiveness. I don't bother counting the number of hours or people our counselors log each month, because I know the process element is meeting a need. Numbers are superfluous in this case.

After you look at the numbers and compare your status quo to your ideal processes, relate these factors to one another, looking for connections between changes in the process and changes in numeric results. An illustration of this can be seen in a conversation with my European friend.

"We're not like you Americans."

"Oh, really. How is that?"

"Our people aren't generous," he replied. "People at our churches don't give."

"When was the last time you did a teaching on tithing?" I asked.

"We don't do that."

There is a correlation between results and process. We can't set numeric goals without also setting process goals. If I want to affect the amount of money given by our congregation, I ought to have a plan to teach on tithing and giving every eighteen to twenty-four months. Preaching on tithing isn't the only process that builds giving. I have also found that when people in our church testify of the miracles God does as they tithe, the giving of the whole congregation increases. So I ask myself how I can inspire people in my church to testify about the blessings of tithing, not just on Sunday morning but one on one during the week.

If you don't evaluate your process goals, you will tend to get locked into simple bean counting, which doesn't help much. Ask yourself, "Has the church process as arranged helped the church accomplish its mission?" Examine each part of the process for effectiveness. While the overall process may not have been as effective as desired, certain parts of the process may have shown promise, while other parts are clearly missing the mark.

In both numeric and process goals, focus on the value added—the difference the church makes—not simply on numbers. Effectiveness is about what actually happens to people who attend a church. Are they changed and helped? What changes occurred in them that would not have occurred otherwise?

A different but overlapping grid for evaluating outcomes is to think in terms of *people results* and *people resources*. What happens *to* the people who attend the church are *people results*. What happens *through* the people who attend the church are *people resources*. People are both results of the process and resources in the process. For example, a people result goal may be a certain number of conversions. But conversions are not enough. These converts must reproduce what has happened in their lives, to win other converts. People results (conversions) are wonderful, but so are people resources (people who witness). Such converts become a resource for more converts. So we need to always be asking ourselves whether we are producing both results and resources. The table below illustrates how these various outcomes overlap.

	People Results	**People Resources**
Numeric Goals	Conversions	People witnessing
	Service attendance	Attenders inviting friends
	Tithes and offering income	Number of people who tithe
	Number of people counseled	Discipling and counseling of friends
Process Goals	Evangelistic sermons, outreach concerts	People giving testimonies, playing in concerts
	Church services, church information material, children's ministries	People as ushers, worship team members
	Stewardship projects, biblical teachings on finances	People testifying and teaching others about tithing
	Prayer teams, counselor training courses	People serving on counseling teams

One of the last stages of evaluation is to determine whether what has been accomplished has been worth the effort to accomplish it. We sometimes put tremendous energy and effort into projects with negligible results. For example, a large, well-organized evangelistic crusade was held in our community a few years ago. All the churches got together and provided volunteers who received training as counselors. The evangelist came into town and held some excellent meetings. Yet after all the work we did, we evaluated the number of new people who ultimately ended up in our church from the crusade. The answer was one person, one person who had previously come to our church a couple of times and at the crusade had recommitted his life to the Lord. He disappeared in three weeks.

Perhaps we didn't do it right. Perhaps other churches in our community contacted hundreds of people who received Christ. If I only had numeric goals, I would definitely wait for a clear go-ahead signal from the Lord before investing similar energy in such an event in the future. But since I also have process goals in mind, I know that what happened *to* the people in my church, the ones who received the counselor training, made them better resources for our future.

What we count is very important. Church leaders have been afraid of evaluation because they have only been able to view church as a production, a single snapshot, a lake. In such static concepts of church, size numbers are the only ones that count. But when church is viewed as a process, marvelous transformations take place in a leader's thinking:

1. Since the church is still in process, it is both unfair and unnecessary to make a final pronouncement about it. Needing more work here or there is not the same as failing. Church as a process removes a leader's fear of failure.

2. Since the church process is fluid and variable, it will need different things at different times. The various resources (for example, people, money, time) of the church must be deployed and rearranged frequently. Church as a process promotes flexibility and change in a leader.

3. Since the church process does things *to* people and *with* them, it does not need to be evaluated by the total number of people in it. Churches can be legitimate despite size—two or three gathered together can make a difference in each other's lives and in the world. Church as a process urges the leader to consider people, not just count them.

4. Since the church process is mostly intangible and immaterial, it does not depend on physical capabilities or attributes of a church (buildings, staff, equipment). What happens between the meetings off campus is more telling than what happens during a production or service on campus. Church as a process equalizes every leader's opportunity to disciple others.

The static production model for church will cause leaders to either resist evaluation out of fear of failure or to spiritualize success with humble-sounding words that offer no point of instruction or help to other leaders who also want to succeed for the Lord. On the other hand, when church leaders evaluate what they and their churches are doing from a process orientation, the analysis will offer them clues about what they might try in order to do an even better job. They can look at the map and decide whether there is a better way to take the passengers to their destination. The river can change course.

Church as a process is church as a promise.

BIBLIOGRAPHY

Barker, Joel A. *Discovering the Future*. St. Paul: Infinity Limited, Inc., 1985.

Bennis, Warren. *On Becoming a Leader*. Reading, Pa.: Addison-Wesley, 1989.

_____. *Why Leaders Can't Lead*. San Francisco: Jossey-Bass, 1990.

Bennis, Warren, and Burt Nanus. *Leaders: The Strategies for Making Change*. San Francisco: Harper and Row, 1985.

Blanchard, Kenneth, and Spencer Johnson. *The One-Minute Manager*. New York: Morrow, 1982.

Bryson, John M. *Strategic Planning for Public and Non-Profit Organizations*. San Francisco: Jossey-Bass, 1988.

Callahan, Kennon L. *Effective Church Leadership*. San Francisco: Harper and Row, 1990.

_____. *Twelve Keys to an Effective Church*. San Francisco: Harper and Row, 1983.

Conger, Jay A. *The Charismatic Leader*. San Francisco: Jossey-Bass, 1989.

Covey, Stephen R. *Principle-Centered Leadership*. Provo, Utah: Institute for Principle-Centered Leadership, 1990.

_____. *The Seven Habits of Highly Effective People*. New York: Simon and Schuster, 1989.

Davis, Stanley M. *Future Perfect*. Reading, Pa.: Addison-Wesley, 1987.

De Pree, Max. *Leadership Is an Art*. New York: Bantam-Doubleday-Dell, 1989.

Dickman, Craig R. *Mind of a Manager, Soul of a Leader*. New York: John Wiley and Sons, 1990.

Drucker, Peter. *Managing the Non-Profit Organization: Principles and Practices*. New York: HarperCollins, 1990.

Ellis, Joe S. *The Church on Purpose.* Cincinnati: Standard, 1982.

Gardner, John W. *On Leadership.* New York: Free Press, 1990.

Gangel, Kenneth O. *Feeding and Leading.* Wheaton, Ill.: Victor Books, 1989.

George, Carl F., and Robert E. Logan. *Leading and Managing Your Church.* New York: Revell, 1987.

_____. *Prepare Your Church for the Future.* New York: Revell, 1991.

Gerber, Michael E. *The E-Myth: Why Most Small Businesses Don't Work.* New York: HarperBusiness, 1986.

Landon, Manual. *Change Agents.* San Francisco: Jossey-Bass, 1988.

Kaufman, Herbert. *Time, Change, and Organizations.* Chatham, N.J.: Chatham Publishers, 1985.

Kouzes, James M., and Barry Z. Posner. *The Leadership Challenge.* San Francisco: Jossey-Bass, 1990.

Mitchell, Kenneth R. *Multiple Staff Ministries.* Philadelphia: Westminster Press, 1988.

Rost, Joseph C. *Leadership for the 21st Century.* New York: Praeger, 1991.

Ruch, Richard S., and Ronald Goodman. *Image at the Top.* New York: Free Press, 1983.

Schein, Edgar H. *Organizational Culture and Leadership.* San Francisco: Jossey-Bass, 1990.

NOTES

Chapter Three: Communicating Vision

[1]Michael E. Gerber, *The E-Myth* (New York: Harper Business, 1986).

[2]Joe S. Ellis, *Managing the Non-Profit Organization* (New York: HarperCollins, 1990), 3.

[3]*The Church on Purpose* (Cincinnati: Standard, 1982), 21.

[4]Max De Pree, *Leadership Is an Art* (New York: Bantam-Doubleday-Dell, 1989).

Chapter Six: Empowering People

[1]Kenneth Blanchard and Spencer Johnson, *The One-Minute Manager* (New York: Morrow, 1982), 19.

Chapter Seven: Adjusting Culture

[1]Edgar H. Schein, *Organizational Culture and Leadership* (San Francisco: Jossey-Bass, 1990), 9.

[2]James M. Kouzes and Barry Z. Posner, *The Leadership Challenge* (San Francisco: Jossey-Bass, 1990), 60–61.

ABOUT DANIEL A. BROWN

Senior Pastor,
The Coastlands—Aptos Foursquare Church

D aniel A. Brown has had a rich history of ministry involvement since his early days in college at UCLA when his "comfortable faith" was challenged and he decided to give everything in service to the Savior he had known since childhood. He led numerous small-group Bible studies for college students while at UCLA from 1970 to 1977, when he completed his M.A. in Literature. After becoming a college instructor at a two-year college, he joined the faculty at LIFE Bible College in Los Angeles in 1978.

In 1979 he joined the pastoral staff of The Church On The Way to oversee and direct the College-Career Ministry. The college group rapidly grew to one of the largest in California, as did a new group for singles ages twenty-five to thirty, which Daniel started in 1980.

Four years later, in December 1984, the Browns led a small company of collegians and young singles from Van Nuys to Aptos, California, to pioneer a new church. Having vacationed with grandparents in Santa Cruz as a boy, and then while in college being moved upon by God to proclaim life to the people of Santa Cruz County, Daniel began the exciting process called The Coastlands.

The confrontation Daniel had with the Jesus of his boyhood, who wanted to become the Lord of his life, has made a lasting and unmistakable impression. The basic message Daniel shares with old and young alike can best be summed up with one of his favorite expressions—"radical obedience"—by which he means complete and utter willingness to follow the slightest urging of the King.

"Nurturing" best describes the thrust of his life and ministry. Foremost in Daniel's teaching and thinking is the concept of developing people, especially leaders, and releasing them in significant ministry. This is evidenced by the fourteen churches The Coastlands has pioneered since 1985, as well as the fifty home-groups that care for its nine hundred weekend attenders.

"Preaching," he says, "should be fun—to listen to and to do." His teaching style has been described as practical, confrontive, and challenging, but Daniel also has a way of lacing humor and drama throughout his messages. Although he holds a Ph.D. from UCLA and is an elected member of Phi Beta Kappa, Daniel stresses the simple truths and refers again and again to "the simplicity and purity of devotion to Christ" (2 Cor. 11:3).

His growing international speaking ministry focuses primarily on pastors' conferences—communicating a practical philosophy of church leadership and discipleship. In 1994 Daniel's first book, *Unlock the Power of Family*, was published by Sparrow Press. He has developed two video teaching series, *Leadership* and *Discipleship*, in conjunction with the Charles E. Fuller Institute in California.

Daniel married his high school sweetheart, Pamela Anne Chevron, in 1973, and they have four children—Hilary, Collin, Lorrel, and Evan.

To contact Daniel Brown or to receive information about audio resources available for pastors and lay leaders:

The Coastlands
280 State Park Drive
Aptos, CA 95073
Telephone: 408-688-5775
Fax: 408-685-3501
e-mail: danielb@coastlands.com
http://www.coastlands.com

We want to hear from you. Please send your comments about this
book to us in care of the address below. Thank you.

ZondervanPublishingHouse
Grand Rapids, Michigan 49530
http://www.zondervan.com